50 Sugar Recipes for Home

By: Kelly Johnson

Table of Contents

- Chocolate Chip Cookies
- Brownies
- Vanilla Cupcakes
- Lemon Bars
- Apple Pie
- Chocolate Cake
- Cheesecake
- Sugar Cookies
- Cinnamon Rolls
- Pecan Pie
- Banana Bread
- Red Velvet Cake
- Carrot Cake
- Coconut Macaroons
- Rice Krispie Treats
- Lemon Meringue Pie
- Strawberry Shortcake
- Cupcake Frosting
- Tiramisu
- Key Lime Pie
- Snickerdoodles
- Pumpkin Pie
- Oatmeal Raisin Cookies
- Peach Cobbler
- Chocolate Brownie Ice Cream Sundae
- Raspberry Jam
- Coconut Cream Pie
- Molasses Cookies
- Apple Crisp
- Chocolate Truffles
- Maple Pecan Bars
- Scones
- French Toast
- Bread Pudding
- Mousse
- Whoopie Pies

- Almond Cake
- Sweet Rolls
- Raspberry Lemon Bars
- Chocolate Eclairs
- Panna Cotta
- Chocolate Fondue
- Granola Bars
- Lemon Glaze
- Coffee Cake
- Strawberry Rhubarb Pie
- Chocolate Soufflé
- Cream Puffs
- Gingerbread Cookies
- Custard

Chocolate Chip Cookies

Ingredients:

- 1 cup (2 sticks) unsalted butter, softened
- 1 cup granulated sugar
- 1 cup packed brown sugar
- 2 large eggs
- 2 teaspoons vanilla extract
- 3 cups all-purpose flour
- 1 teaspoon baking soda
- 1/2 teaspoon baking powder
- 1/2 teaspoon salt
- 2 cups semi-sweet chocolate chips

Instructions:

1. **Preheat Oven**: Preheat your oven to 350°F (175°C). Line baking sheets with parchment paper or silicone baking mats.
2. **Cream Butter and Sugars**: In a large bowl, use an electric mixer to cream together the softened butter, granulated sugar, and brown sugar until light and fluffy.
3. **Add Eggs and Vanilla**: Beat in the eggs one at a time, mixing well after each addition. Then, mix in the vanilla extract.
4. **Mix Dry Ingredients**: In a separate bowl, whisk together the flour, baking soda, baking powder, and salt.
5. **Combine Mixtures**: Gradually add the dry ingredients to the wet ingredients, mixing until just combined. Be careful not to overmix.
6. **Add Chocolate Chips**: Fold in the chocolate chips using a spatula or wooden spoon.
7. **Scoop Dough**: Drop rounded tablespoons of dough onto the prepared baking sheets, spacing them about 2 inches apart.
8. **Bake**: Bake in the preheated oven for 10-12 minutes, or until the edges are golden brown but the centers are still soft.
9. **Cool**: Allow cookies to cool on the baking sheets for a few minutes before transferring them to wire racks to cool completely.

Enjoy your freshly baked chocolate chip cookies!

Brownies

Ingredients:

- 1/2 cup (1 stick) unsalted butter
- 1 cup granulated sugar
- 2 large eggs
- 1 teaspoon vanilla extract
- 1/3 cup unsweetened cocoa powder
- 1/2 cup all-purpose flour
- 1/4 teaspoon salt
- 1/4 teaspoon baking powder
- 1/2 cup chocolate chips (optional)

Instructions:

1. **Preheat Oven**: Preheat your oven to 350°F (175°C). Grease an 8x8-inch baking pan or line it with parchment paper.
2. **Melt Butter**: In a medium saucepan, melt the butter over low heat. Remove from heat and stir in the granulated sugar, eggs, and vanilla extract until well combined.
3. **Mix Dry Ingredients**: In a separate bowl, whisk together the cocoa powder, flour, salt, and baking powder.
4. **Combine Ingredients**: Gradually stir the dry ingredients into the wet ingredients until just combined. If using chocolate chips, fold them in at this point.
5. **Pour Batter**: Pour the brownie batter into the prepared baking pan and spread it evenly.
6. **Bake**: Bake in the preheated oven for 20-25 minutes, or until a toothpick inserted into the center comes out with a few moist crumbs. The brownies should be set around the edges but still slightly gooey in the middle.
7. **Cool**: Allow the brownies to cool in the pan on a wire rack before cutting them into squares.

Enjoy your homemade brownies!

Vanilla Cupcakes

Ingredients:

For the Cupcakes:

- 1 1/2 cups all-purpose flour
- 1 cup granulated sugar
- 1/2 cup unsalted butter, softened
- 1/2 cup milk (whole or 2%)
- 2 large eggs
- 2 teaspoons vanilla extract
- 1 1/2 teaspoons baking powder
- 1/4 teaspoon salt

For the Frosting:

- 1/2 cup (1 stick) unsalted butter, softened
- 2 cups powdered sugar
- 2 tablespoons milk
- 1 teaspoon vanilla extract

Instructions:

1. Preheat Oven:

- Preheat your oven to 350°F (175°C). Line a 12-cup muffin tin with cupcake liners.

2. Mix Dry Ingredients:

- In a medium bowl, whisk together the flour, baking powder, and salt. Set aside.

3. Cream Butter and Sugar:

- In a large bowl, use an electric mixer to cream the softened butter and granulated sugar together until light and fluffy.

4. Add Eggs and Vanilla:

- Beat in the eggs one at a time, mixing well after each addition. Then, mix in the vanilla extract.

5. Combine Ingredients:

- Gradually add the dry ingredients to the butter mixture, alternating with the milk. Begin and end with the dry ingredients, mixing until just combined. Be careful not to overmix.

6. Fill Cupcake Liners:

- Divide the batter evenly among the cupcake liners, filling each about 2/3 full.

7. Bake:

- Bake in the preheated oven for 18-20 minutes, or until a toothpick inserted into the center of a cupcake comes out clean.

8. Cool:

- Allow the cupcakes to cool in the tin for 5 minutes, then transfer them to a wire rack to cool completely before frosting.

9. Make Frosting:

- While the cupcakes are cooling, make the frosting. In a large bowl, beat the softened butter with an electric mixer until creamy. Gradually add the powdered sugar, mixing on low speed until combined. Add the milk and vanilla extract and beat until smooth and fluffy.

10. Frost Cupcakes:

- Once the cupcakes are completely cool, frost them with the vanilla frosting using a knife or a piping bag.

Enjoy your homemade vanilla cupcakes!

Lemon Bars

Ingredients:

For the Crust:

- 1 3/4 cups all-purpose flour
- 1/2 cup granulated sugar
- 1/2 cup (1 stick) unsalted butter, cold and cut into small pieces
- 1/4 teaspoon salt

For the Lemon Filling:

- 1 cup granulated sugar
- 2 tablespoons all-purpose flour
- 1/2 teaspoon baking powder
- 1/4 teaspoon salt
- 4 large eggs
- 1/2 cup fresh lemon juice (about 2-3 lemons)
- Zest of 1 lemon (optional)
- Powdered sugar, for dusting (optional)

Instructions:

1. Preheat Oven:

- Preheat your oven to 350°F (175°C). Grease and flour an 8x8-inch baking pan or line it with parchment paper.

2. Prepare the Crust:

- In a medium bowl, mix together the flour, granulated sugar, and salt. Cut in the cold butter using a pastry cutter or your fingers until the mixture resembles coarse crumbs.

3. Bake the Crust:

- Press the mixture evenly into the bottom of the prepared pan. Bake in the preheated oven for 15-18 minutes, or until the edges are lightly golden.

4. Prepare the Lemon Filling:

- While the crust is baking, in a medium bowl, whisk together the granulated sugar, flour, baking powder, and salt.
- In a separate bowl, beat the eggs, then whisk in the lemon juice and lemon zest if using.

5. Combine and Bake:

- Gradually add the dry ingredients to the wet ingredients, mixing until smooth. Pour the lemon mixture over the pre-baked crust.

6. Bake Lemon Bars:

- Return the pan to the oven and bake for an additional 20-25 minutes, or until the filling is set and no longer jiggles in the center.

7. Cool and Serve:

- Allow the lemon bars to cool completely in the pan on a wire rack. Once cooled, dust with powdered sugar if desired, then cut into squares.

Enjoy your tangy, sweet lemon bars!

Apple Pie

Ingredients:

For the Pie Crust:

- 2 1/2 cups all-purpose flour
- 1 cup (2 sticks) unsalted butter, cold and cut into small pieces
- 1/4 cup granulated sugar
- 1/4 teaspoon salt
- 6-8 tablespoons ice water

For the Apple Filling:

- 6-7 cups peeled, cored, and sliced apples (Granny Smith, Honeycrisp, or a mix)
- 3/4 cup granulated sugar
- 1/4 cup packed brown sugar
- 1/4 cup all-purpose flour
- 1 teaspoon ground cinnamon
- 1/4 teaspoon ground nutmeg
- 1/4 teaspoon salt
- 1 tablespoon lemon juice (about 1/2 lemon)
- 1 tablespoon unsalted butter, cut into small pieces
- 1 large egg, beaten (for egg wash)
- 1 tablespoon granulated sugar (for sprinkling)

Instructions:

1. Prepare the Pie Crust:

- In a large bowl, combine the flour, granulated sugar, and salt.
- Add the cold butter pieces and cut them into the flour mixture using a pastry cutter or your fingers until the mixture resembles coarse crumbs.
- Gradually add ice water, 1 tablespoon at a time, mixing until the dough just comes together. You may not need all the water.
- Divide the dough into two equal portions, shape each into a disc, wrap in plastic wrap, and refrigerate for at least 1 hour.

2. Prepare the Apple Filling:

- In a large bowl, toss the sliced apples with lemon juice.
- In a separate bowl, mix the granulated sugar, brown sugar, flour, cinnamon, nutmeg, and salt.
- Add the sugar mixture to the apples and toss to coat.

3. Assemble the Pie:

- Preheat your oven to 425°F (220°C).
- On a lightly floured surface, roll out one disc of dough to fit a 9-inch pie pan. Transfer the rolled-out dough to the pie pan and trim the edges.
- Pour the apple filling into the crust and dot with small pieces of butter.
- Roll out the second disc of dough and place it over the apple filling. Trim and crimp the edges to seal the pie. Cut slits or create a lattice pattern in the top crust to allow steam to escape.
- Brush the top crust with the beaten egg and sprinkle with granulated sugar.

4. Bake the Pie:

- Bake in the preheated oven for 45-55 minutes, or until the crust is golden brown and the filling is bubbling.
- If the edges of the crust start to brown too quickly, cover them with foil or a pie shield.

5. Cool and Serve:

- Allow the pie to cool on a wire rack for at least 2 hours before serving. This allows the filling to set properly.

Enjoy your homemade apple pie with a scoop of vanilla ice cream or a dollop of whipped cream!

Chocolate Cake

Ingredients:

For the Cake:

- 1 3/4 cups all-purpose flour
- 1 1/2 cups granulated sugar
- 3/4 cup unsweetened cocoa powder
- 1 1/2 teaspoons baking powder
- 1 1/2 teaspoons baking soda
- 1/2 teaspoon salt
- 2 large eggs
- 1 cup whole milk
- 1/2 cup vegetable oil
- 2 teaspoons vanilla extract
- 1 cup boiling water

For the Chocolate Frosting:

- 1 cup (2 sticks) unsalted butter, softened
- 3 1/2 cups powdered sugar
- 1/2 cup unsweetened cocoa powder
- 1/4 cup whole milk (or more, as needed)
- 2 teaspoons vanilla extract
- A pinch of salt

Instructions:

1. Preheat Oven:

- Preheat your oven to 350°F (175°C). Grease and flour two 9-inch round cake pans, or line them with parchment paper.

2. Mix Dry Ingredients:

- In a large bowl, sift together the flour, granulated sugar, cocoa powder, baking powder, baking soda, and salt.

3. Mix Wet Ingredients:

- In a separate bowl, beat the eggs. Add the milk, vegetable oil, and vanilla extract, and mix well.

4. Combine Ingredients:

- Gradually add the wet ingredients to the dry ingredients, mixing until just combined.
- Carefully stir in the boiling water. The batter will be thin, but that's okay; it helps create a moist cake.

5. Bake the Cake:

- Divide the batter evenly between the prepared cake pans.
- Bake in the preheated oven for 30-35 minutes, or until a toothpick inserted into the center comes out clean.

6. Cool:

- Allow the cakes to cool in the pans for 10 minutes, then transfer them to a wire rack to cool completely before frosting.

7. Make the Frosting:

- In a large bowl, beat the softened butter until creamy.
- Gradually add the powdered sugar and cocoa powder, beating on low speed until combined.
- Add the milk, vanilla extract, and a pinch of salt. Beat on high speed until light and fluffy. If the frosting is too thick, add a bit more milk. If it's too thin, add a little more powdered sugar.

8. Frost the Cake:

- Once the cakes are completely cool, spread a layer of frosting on top of one cake layer. Place the second layer on top and frost the top and sides of the cake.

Enjoy your delicious homemade chocolate cake!

Cheesecake

Ingredients:

For the Crust:

- 1 1/2 cups graham cracker crumbs (about 10-12 graham crackers, crushed)
- 1/4 cup granulated sugar
- 1/2 cup (1 stick) unsalted butter, melted

For the Cheesecake Filling:

- 4 (8-ounce) packages cream cheese, softened
- 1 cup granulated sugar
- 1 teaspoon vanilla extract
- 4 large eggs
- 1 cup sour cream
- 1 cup heavy cream

For the Topping (Optional):

- Fresh fruit, fruit compote, or chocolate ganache

Instructions:

1. Prepare the Crust:

- Preheat your oven to 325°F (163°C).
- In a medium bowl, combine the graham cracker crumbs, granulated sugar, and melted butter. Mix until the crumbs are evenly coated and the mixture resembles wet sand.
- Press the mixture into the bottom of a 9-inch springform pan, creating an even layer.

2. Bake the Crust:

- Bake the crust in the preheated oven for 10 minutes. Remove from the oven and let it cool while you prepare the filling.

3. Prepare the Cheesecake Filling:

- In a large mixing bowl, beat the softened cream cheese with an electric mixer until smooth and creamy.
- Add the granulated sugar and vanilla extract. Beat until well combined.
- Add the eggs, one at a time, mixing well after each addition.
- Mix in the sour cream and heavy cream until the batter is smooth and well combined.

4. Bake the Cheesecake:

- Pour the cheesecake batter over the cooled crust in the springform pan.
- Smooth the top with a spatula.
- Bake in the preheated oven for 55-65 minutes, or until the center is set and the edges are slightly puffed. The center should still have a slight jiggle.

5. Cool the Cheesecake:

- Turn off the oven and crack the oven door. Let the cheesecake cool in the oven for 1 hour to prevent cracking.
- After 1 hour, remove the cheesecake from the oven and let it cool completely at room temperature.
- Once cooled, refrigerate the cheesecake for at least 4 hours or overnight to allow it to set properly.

6. Add Toppings:

- Before serving, top the cheesecake with fresh fruit, fruit compote, or chocolate ganache if desired.

7. Serve:

- Remove the cheesecake from the springform pan and transfer it to a serving plate.
- Slice and serve chilled.

Enjoy your homemade cheesecake!

Sugar Cookies

Ingredients:

- 2 3/4 cups all-purpose flour
- 1 1/2 teaspoons baking powder
- 1/2 teaspoon salt
- 1 cup (2 sticks) unsalted butter, softened
- 1 1/2 cups granulated sugar
- 1 large egg
- 1 teaspoon vanilla extract
- 1/2 teaspoon almond extract (optional)
- Additional granulated sugar or colored sugar for rolling (optional)

Instructions:

1. Preheat Oven:

- Preheat your oven to 350°F (175°C). Line baking sheets with parchment paper or silicone baking mats.

2. Mix Dry Ingredients:

- In a medium bowl, whisk together the flour, baking powder, and salt. Set aside.

3. Cream Butter and Sugar:

- In a large bowl, use an electric mixer to cream the softened butter and granulated sugar together until light and fluffy.

4. Add Egg and Extracts:

- Beat in the egg, vanilla extract, and almond extract (if using) until well combined.

5. Combine Ingredients:

- Gradually add the dry ingredients to the wet ingredients, mixing on low speed until just combined. The dough should come together and be slightly soft but not sticky.

6. Roll and Cut Cookies:

- On a lightly floured surface, roll out the dough to about 1/4 inch thick. Use cookie cutters to cut out shapes. If desired, sprinkle a little granulated sugar or colored sugar on top of each cookie before baking.

7. Bake:

- Place the cut-out cookies on the prepared baking sheets, spacing them about 1 inch apart.
- Bake in the preheated oven for 8-10 minutes, or until the edges are lightly golden. The centers should still be soft.

8. Cool:

- Allow the cookies to cool on the baking sheets for a few minutes before transferring them to a wire rack to cool completely.

9. Decorate (Optional):

- Once the cookies are completely cooled, you can decorate them with royal icing, colored sugar, or sprinkles if desired.

Enjoy your homemade sugar cookies!

Cinnamon Rolls

Ingredients:

For the Dough:

- 1 cup whole milk
- 1/4 cup granulated sugar
- 1/4 cup unsalted butter
- 2 1/4 teaspoons active dry yeast (1 packet)
- 2 large eggs
- 4 cups all-purpose flour
- 1/2 teaspoon salt

For the Filling:

- 1/2 cup unsalted butter, softened
- 1 cup packed brown sugar
- 2 tablespoons ground cinnamon

For the Cream Cheese Frosting:

- 4 ounces cream cheese, softened
- 1/4 cup unsalted butter, softened
- 1 1/2 cups powdered sugar
- 1/2 teaspoon vanilla extract
- 1-2 tablespoons milk (if needed)

Instructions:

1. Prepare the Dough:

- Heat the milk in a saucepan over medium heat until it's warm (about 110°F/43°C). Remove from heat and stir in the granulated sugar and butter until the butter is melted.
- Sprinkle the yeast over the milk mixture and let it sit for about 5 minutes, or until it becomes frothy.
- In a large bowl, beat the eggs and add them to the yeast mixture.
- Gradually add the flour and salt, mixing until a dough forms. The dough should be soft but not sticky. You may need to adjust the amount of flour slightly.

2. Knead and Rise:

- Turn the dough out onto a floured surface and knead for about 5 minutes, or until smooth and elastic.
- Place the dough in a lightly greased bowl, cover it with a damp cloth or plastic wrap, and let it rise in a warm place for about 1 to 1 1/2 hours, or until doubled in size.

3. Prepare the Filling:

- In a medium bowl, mix together the softened butter, brown sugar, and cinnamon until well combined.

4. Roll Out the Dough:

- Punch down the risen dough and turn it out onto a floured surface. Roll it into a rectangle about 16x12 inches.
- Spread the cinnamon filling evenly over the dough, leaving a small border around the edges.

5. Roll and Cut:

- Roll the dough tightly from the long side, forming a log. Pinch the edges to seal.
- Cut the rolled dough into 12-15 equal slices and place them in a greased 9x13-inch baking pan or on a parchment-lined baking sheet.

6. Second Rise:

- Cover the rolls with a damp cloth or plastic wrap and let them rise in a warm place for about 30 minutes, or until puffy.

7. Bake:

- Preheat your oven to 350°F (175°C).
- Bake the cinnamon rolls for 20-25 minutes, or until golden brown.

8. Prepare the Cream Cheese Frosting:

- While the rolls are baking, beat together the cream cheese and butter in a medium bowl until creamy.
- Gradually add the powdered sugar and vanilla extract, mixing until smooth. If needed, add milk a tablespoon at a time until the frosting reaches your desired consistency.

9. Frost and Serve:

- Once the rolls are baked and still warm, spread the cream cheese frosting over them.
- Serve warm and enjoy!

These cinnamon rolls are perfect for breakfast or a sweet treat any time of the day!

Pecan Pie

Ingredients:

For the Pie Crust:

- 1 1/4 cups all-purpose flour
- 1/4 teaspoon salt
- 1/2 cup (1 stick) unsalted butter, cold and cut into small pieces
- 1/4 cup granulated sugar
- 1/4 cup ice water (more if needed)

For the Filling:

- 1 cup light corn syrup
- 1 cup packed brown sugar
- 1/2 cup unsalted butter, melted
- 4 large eggs
- 1 1/2 teaspoons vanilla extract
- 1/4 teaspoon salt
- 1 1/2 cups pecan halves

Instructions:

1. Prepare the Pie Crust:

- In a medium bowl, combine the flour and salt. Cut in the cold butter using a pastry cutter or your fingers until the mixture resembles coarse crumbs.
- Stir in the granulated sugar.
- Gradually add ice water, one tablespoon at a time, mixing until the dough comes together. You may need more or less water depending on the humidity.
- Shape the dough into a disc, wrap it in plastic wrap, and refrigerate for at least 1 hour.

2. Preheat Oven:

- Preheat your oven to 350°F (175°C).

3. Roll Out the Dough:

- On a lightly floured surface, roll out the chilled dough to fit a 9-inch pie pan. Transfer the dough to the pan and trim any excess, crimping the edges as desired.
- Place the pie crust in the refrigerator while you prepare the filling.

4. Prepare the Filling:

- In a large bowl, whisk together the corn syrup, brown sugar, melted butter, eggs, vanilla extract, and salt until smooth and well combined.
- Stir in the pecan halves.

5. Assemble the Pie:

- Pour the pecan filling into the prepared pie crust. Spread the pecans evenly.

6. Bake:

- Bake the pie in the preheated oven for 50-60 minutes, or until the filling is set and the crust is golden brown. If the crust starts to brown too quickly, cover the edges with aluminum foil to prevent burning.
- The center of the pie should be slightly jiggly but will set as it cools.

7. Cool:

- Allow the pie to cool completely on a wire rack before slicing. This helps the filling to firm up and makes it easier to cut.

Enjoy your homemade pecan pie!

Banana Bread

Ingredients:

For the Pie Crust:

- 1 1/4 cups all-purpose flour
- 1/4 teaspoon salt
- 1/2 cup (1 stick) unsalted butter, cold and cut into small pieces
- 1/4 cup granulated sugar
- 1/4 cup ice water (more if needed)

For the Filling:

- 1 cup light corn syrup
- 1 cup packed brown sugar
- 1/2 cup unsalted butter, melted
- 4 large eggs
- 1 1/2 teaspoons vanilla extract
- 1/4 teaspoon salt
- 1 1/2 cups pecan halves

Instructions:

1. Prepare the Pie Crust:

- In a medium bowl, combine the flour and salt. Cut in the cold butter using a pastry cutter or your fingers until the mixture resembles coarse crumbs.
- Stir in the granulated sugar.
- Gradually add ice water, one tablespoon at a time, mixing until the dough comes together. You may need more or less water depending on the humidity.
- Shape the dough into a disc, wrap it in plastic wrap, and refrigerate for at least 1 hour.

2. Preheat Oven:

- Preheat your oven to 350°F (175°C).

3. Roll Out the Dough:

- On a lightly floured surface, roll out the chilled dough to fit a 9-inch pie pan. Transfer the dough to the pan and trim any excess, crimping the edges as desired.
- Place the pie crust in the refrigerator while you prepare the filling.

4. Prepare the Filling:

- In a large bowl, whisk together the corn syrup, brown sugar, melted butter, eggs, vanilla extract, and salt until smooth and well combined.
- Stir in the pecan halves.

5. Assemble the Pie:

- Pour the pecan filling into the prepared pie crust. Spread the pecans evenly.

6. Bake:

- Bake the pie in the preheated oven for 50-60 minutes, or until the filling is set and the crust is golden brown. If the crust starts to brown too quickly, cover the edges with aluminum foil to prevent burning.
- The center of the pie should be slightly jiggly but will set as it cools.

7. Cool:

- Allow the pie to cool completely on a wire rack before slicing. This helps the filling to firm up and makes it easier to cut.

Enjoy your homemade pecan pie!

Banana Bread

Ingredients:

- 1 1/2 cups all-purpose flour
- 1 teaspoon baking powder
- 1/2 teaspoon baking soda
- 1/4 teaspoon salt
- 1/2 cup (1 stick) unsalted butter, softened
- 1 cup granulated sugar
- 2 large eggs
- 4 ripe bananas, mashed (about 1 1/2 cups)
- 1 teaspoon vanilla extract
- 1/2 cup chopped nuts or chocolate chips (optional)

Instructions:

1. Preheat Oven:

- Preheat your oven to 350°F (175°C). Grease and flour a 9x5-inch loaf pan or line it with parchment paper.

2. Mix Dry Ingredients:

- In a medium bowl, whisk together the flour, baking powder, baking soda, and salt. Set aside.

3. Cream Butter and Sugar:

- In a large bowl, use an electric mixer to cream the softened butter and granulated sugar together until light and fluffy.

4. Add Eggs and Bananas:

- Beat in the eggs, one at a time, mixing well after each addition.
- Stir in the mashed bananas and vanilla extract until well combined.

5. Combine Ingredients:

- Gradually add the dry ingredients to the wet ingredients, mixing until just combined. Be careful not to overmix.
- If using, fold in the chopped nuts or chocolate chips.

6. Pour Batter:

- Pour the batter into the prepared loaf pan and spread it evenly.

7. Bake:

- Bake in the preheated oven for 60-70 minutes, or until a toothpick inserted into the center comes out clean. The top should be golden brown.

8. Cool:

- Allow the banana bread to cool in the pan for about 10 minutes before transferring it to a wire rack to cool completely.

Enjoy your homemade banana bread with a cup of coffee or tea!

Red Velvet Cake

Ingredients:

For the Cake:

- 2 1/2 cups all-purpose flour
- 1 1/2 cups granulated sugar
- 1 teaspoon baking powder
- 1 teaspoon baking soda
- 1/2 teaspoon salt
- 1 cup vegetable oil
- 1 cup buttermilk, room temperature
- 2 large eggs, room temperature
- 2 tablespoons cocoa powder
- 2 tablespoons red food coloring (liquid or gel)
- 1 teaspoon vanilla extract
- 1 teaspoon white vinegar

For the Cream Cheese Frosting:

- 8 ounces cream cheese, softened
- 1/2 cup unsalted butter, softened
- 4 cups powdered sugar
- 1 teaspoon vanilla extract

Instructions:

1. Preheat Oven:

- Preheat your oven to 350°F (175°C). Grease and flour two 9-inch round cake pans, or line them with parchment paper.

2. Mix Dry Ingredients:

- In a medium bowl, sift together the flour, sugar, baking powder, baking soda, and salt. Set aside.

3. Mix Wet Ingredients:

- In a large bowl, whisk together the oil, buttermilk, eggs, cocoa powder, red food coloring, vanilla extract, and vinegar until well combined.

4. Combine Ingredients:

- Gradually add the dry ingredients to the wet ingredients, mixing on low speed until just combined. Be careful not to overmix.

5. Bake the Cake:

- Divide the batter evenly between the prepared cake pans.
- Bake in the preheated oven for 25-30 minutes, or until a toothpick inserted into the center comes out clean.

6. Cool:

- Allow the cakes to cool in the pans for 10 minutes before transferring them to a wire rack to cool completely.

7. Prepare the Cream Cheese Frosting:

- In a large bowl, beat the softened cream cheese and butter together until creamy and smooth.
- Gradually add the powdered sugar, mixing on low speed until combined.
- Mix in the vanilla extract.

8. Frost the Cake:

- Once the cakes are completely cool, spread a layer of cream cheese frosting on top of one cake layer. Place the second layer on top and frost the top and sides of the cake.

9. Decorate (Optional):

- Decorate with additional frosting, sprinkles, or decorative elements as desired.

Enjoy your homemade Red Velvet Cake with its rich flavor and creamy frosting!

Carrot Cake

Ingredients:

For the Carrot Cake:

- 2 cups all-purpose flour
- 1 1/2 teaspoons baking powder
- 1 1/2 teaspoons baking soda
- 1/2 teaspoon salt
- 2 teaspoons ground cinnamon
- 1/2 teaspoon ground nutmeg
- 1/2 teaspoon ground ginger
- 1 cup vegetable oil
- 1 cup granulated sugar
- 1/2 cup packed brown sugar
- 4 large eggs
- 2 cups grated carrots (about 4 medium carrots)
- 1/2 cup crushed pineapple, drained
- 1/2 cup chopped walnuts or pecans (optional)
- 1/2 cup shredded coconut (optional)
- 1 teaspoon vanilla extract

For the Cream Cheese Frosting:

- 8 ounces cream cheese, softened
- 1/2 cup unsalted butter, softened
- 4 cups powdered sugar
- 1 teaspoon vanilla extract

Instructions:

1. Preheat Oven:

- Preheat your oven to 350°F (175°C). Grease and flour two 9-inch round cake pans or line them with parchment paper.

2. Mix Dry Ingredients:

- In a medium bowl, whisk together the flour, baking powder, baking soda, salt, cinnamon, nutmeg, and ginger. Set aside.

3. Mix Wet Ingredients:

- In a large bowl, beat together the oil, granulated sugar, and brown sugar until well combined.

- Add the eggs, one at a time, beating well after each addition.

4. Combine Ingredients:

- Gradually add the dry ingredients to the wet ingredients, mixing until just combined.
- Fold in the grated carrots, crushed pineapple, chopped nuts (if using), shredded coconut (if using), and vanilla extract.

5. Bake the Cake:

- Divide the batter evenly between the prepared cake pans.
- Bake in the preheated oven for 30-35 minutes, or until a toothpick inserted into the center comes out clean.

6. Cool:

- Allow the cakes to cool in the pans for 10 minutes, then transfer them to a wire rack to cool completely.

7. Prepare the Cream Cheese Frosting:

- In a large bowl, beat together the softened cream cheese and butter until creamy and smooth.
- Gradually add the powdered sugar, mixing on low speed until combined.
- Mix in the vanilla extract.

8. Frost the Cake:

- Once the cakes are completely cooled, spread a layer of cream cheese frosting on top of one cake layer. Place the second layer on top and frost the top and sides of the cake.

9. Decorate (Optional):

- Decorate with additional chopped nuts, shredded coconut, or a sprinkle of cinnamon if desired.

Enjoy your homemade carrot cake with its rich, spiced flavor and creamy frosting!

Coconut Macaroons

Ingredients:

- 4 large egg whites
- 1 cup granulated sugar
- 1/4 teaspoon salt
- 1/2 teaspoon vanilla extract
- 3 1/2 cups sweetened shredded coconut
- 1/4 cup all-purpose flour (optional, for binding)

For the Chocolate Dip (Optional):

- 1 cup semi-sweet chocolate chips
- 1 tablespoon coconut oil or vegetable oil

Instructions:

1. Preheat Oven:

- Preheat your oven to 325°F (165°C). Line a baking sheet with parchment paper or a silicone baking mat.

2. Whip Egg Whites:

- In a large, clean mixing bowl, use an electric mixer to beat the egg whites until they start to foam.
- Add the salt and continue to beat until soft peaks form.

3. Add Sugar and Vanilla:

- Gradually add the granulated sugar to the egg whites, beating on high speed until stiff, glossy peaks form.
- Beat in the vanilla extract.

4. Fold in Coconut:

- Gently fold the shredded coconut into the whipped egg whites until evenly combined. If using flour, add it at this stage and mix until well incorporated.

5. Shape Macaroons:

- Using a small cookie scoop or two spoons, drop spoonfuls of the coconut mixture onto the prepared baking sheet, spacing them about 1 inch apart.

6. Bake:

- Bake in the preheated oven for 15-20 minutes, or until the edges are golden brown and the tops are lightly toasted.

7. Cool:

- Allow the macaroons to cool on the baking sheet for a few minutes before transferring them to a wire rack to cool completely.

8. (Optional) Dip in Chocolate:

- In a small bowl, melt the chocolate chips and coconut oil together in the microwave in 30-second intervals, stirring after each interval until smooth.
- Dip the bottoms of the cooled macaroons into the melted chocolate, allowing any excess to drip off.
- Place the dipped macaroons back on the parchment paper to set until the chocolate is firm.

Enjoy your homemade coconut macaroons, whether you enjoy them plain or dipped in chocolate!

Rice Krispie Treats

Ingredients:

- 6 cups Rice Krispies cereal
- 3 tablespoons unsalted butter
- 1 package (10 ounces) mini marshmallows (or about 6 cups regular marshmallows)
- 1/2 teaspoon vanilla extract (optional)
- A pinch of salt (optional)

Instructions:

1. Prepare Pan:

- Grease a 9x13-inch baking pan with butter or cooking spray. Alternatively, you can line it with parchment paper for easier removal.

2. Melt Butter and Marshmallows:

- In a large saucepan, melt the butter over medium-low heat.
- Add the marshmallows to the melted butter and stir continuously until the marshmallows are completely melted and smooth. If using vanilla extract, stir it in once the marshmallows are melted.

3. Mix with Cereal:

- Remove the saucepan from the heat.
- Quickly add the Rice Krispies cereal to the melted marshmallow mixture, stirring until the cereal is evenly coated.

4. Transfer to Pan:

- Pour the mixture into the prepared baking pan.
- Using a buttered spatula or the back of a spoon, press the mixture evenly into the pan. Be gentle to avoid crushing the cereal.

5. Cool and Cut:

- Allow the Rice Krispie treats to cool completely in the pan before cutting them into squares or rectangles.

6. Serve:

- Enjoy your Rice Krispie Treats once they have set and are cut into pieces.

Feel free to add mix-ins like chocolate chips, peanut butter, or M&Ms if you want to customize your treats!

Lemon Meringue Pie

Ingredients:

For the Pie Crust:

- 1 1/2 cups all-purpose flour
- 1/4 teaspoon salt
- 1/2 cup (1 stick) unsalted butter, cold and cut into small pieces
- 1/4 cup granulated sugar
- 1/4 cup ice water (more if needed)

For the Lemon Filling:

- 1 cup granulated sugar
- 1/4 cup cornstarch
- 1/4 teaspoon salt
- 1 1/2 cups water
- 3 large egg yolks, lightly beaten
- 1/2 cup fresh lemon juice (about 2-3 lemons)
- 2 tablespoons unsalted butter
- 1 tablespoon lemon zest (optional)

For the Meringue:

- 4 large egg whites
- 1/4 teaspoon cream of tartar
- 1/2 cup granulated sugar
- 1/2 teaspoon vanilla extract

Instructions:

1. Prepare the Pie Crust:

- In a medium bowl, combine the flour and salt. Cut in the cold butter using a pastry cutter or your fingers until the mixture resembles coarse crumbs.
- Stir in the granulated sugar.
- Gradually add the ice water, one tablespoon at a time, mixing until the dough comes together. You may need more or less water depending on the humidity.
- Shape the dough into a disc, wrap it in plastic wrap, and refrigerate for at least 1 hour.

2. Preheat Oven:

- Preheat your oven to 375°F (190°C).

3. Roll Out and Bake the Crust:

- On a floured surface, roll out the chilled dough to fit a 9-inch pie pan. Transfer the dough to the pan and trim any excess, crimping the edges as desired.
- Line the crust with parchment paper or aluminum foil and fill with pie weights or dried beans.
- Bake for 15 minutes. Remove the weights and lining and bake for an additional 5-7 minutes, or until the crust is golden brown. Let it cool completely.

4. Prepare the Lemon Filling:

- In a medium saucepan, whisk together the sugar, cornstarch, and salt.
- Gradually whisk in the water until smooth.
- Cook over medium heat, stirring constantly, until the mixture comes to a boil and thickens.
- Reduce heat and cook for 1 more minute, stirring constantly.
- Remove from heat and gradually whisk a small amount of the hot mixture into the beaten egg yolks to temper them.
- Return the egg yolk mixture to the saucepan, whisking constantly. Cook for 1-2 more minutes.
- Remove from heat and stir in the lemon juice, butter, and lemon zest (if using) until well combined and smooth.
- Pour the lemon filling into the cooled pie crust.

5. Prepare the Meringue:

- In a large bowl, beat the egg whites with cream of tartar until soft peaks form.
- Gradually add the granulated sugar, continuing to beat until stiff, glossy peaks form.
- Beat in the vanilla extract.

6. Top the Pie with Meringue:

- Spread the meringue over the lemon filling, making sure to seal the edges to the crust to prevent shrinking.
- Use a spatula to create peaks and swirls in the meringue.

7. Bake:

- Bake the pie in the preheated oven for 10-12 minutes, or until the meringue is golden brown.

8. Cool:

- Allow the pie to cool at room temperature for several hours before slicing. This helps the lemon filling set properly.

Enjoy your homemade Lemon Meringue Pie with its tangy filling and sweet, fluffy meringue!

Strawberry Shortcake

Ingredients:

For the Shortcakes:

- 2 cups all-purpose flour
- 1/4 cup granulated sugar
- 1 tablespoon baking powder
- 1/2 teaspoon salt
- 1/2 cup (1 stick) unsalted butter, cold and cut into small pieces
- 2/3 cup whole milk (more if needed)
- 1 teaspoon vanilla extract

For the Strawberries:

- 1 quart fresh strawberries, hulled and sliced
- 1/4 cup granulated sugar (adjust to taste)

For the Whipped Cream:

- 1 cup heavy cream
- 2 tablespoons granulated sugar
- 1 teaspoon vanilla extract

Instructions:

1. Prepare the Strawberries:

- In a medium bowl, toss the sliced strawberries with the granulated sugar.
- Let them sit for about 30 minutes to an hour to release their juices and become syrupy.

2. Preheat Oven:

- Preheat your oven to 425°F (220°C). Line a baking sheet with parchment paper.

3. Make the Shortcakes:

- In a large bowl, whisk together the flour, sugar, baking powder, and salt.
- Cut in the cold butter using a pastry cutter or your fingers until the mixture resembles coarse crumbs.
- Stir in the milk and vanilla extract just until combined. The dough should be soft but not too sticky. If needed, add a little more milk.
- Turn the dough out onto a floured surface and gently pat it to about 1-inch thickness.
- Use a round cutter (about 2.5 to 3 inches in diameter) to cut out shortcakes. Re-roll the scraps if necessary.

4. Bake the Shortcakes:

- Place the shortcakes on the prepared baking sheet.
- Bake in the preheated oven for 12-15 minutes, or until they are golden brown.
- Remove from the oven and let them cool on a wire rack.

5. Prepare the Whipped Cream:

- In a large bowl, beat the heavy cream with an electric mixer until it starts to thicken.
- Add the sugar and vanilla extract.
- Continue to beat until stiff peaks form.

6. Assemble the Strawberry Shortcakes:

- Slice the cooled shortcakes in half horizontally.
- Spoon a generous amount of the sugared strawberries over the bottom half of each shortcake.
- Top with a dollop of whipped cream.
- Place the top half of the shortcake over the whipped cream.

7. Serve:

- Serve the Strawberry Shortcakes immediately, garnished with extra strawberries and whipped cream if desired.

Enjoy your homemade Strawberry Shortcake, perfect for a light and delicious dessert!

Cupcake Frosting

Ingredients:

- 1 cup (2 sticks) unsalted butter, softened
- 3-4 cups powdered sugar
- 2 tablespoons heavy cream or milk
- 1 teaspoon vanilla extract
- A pinch of salt (optional)

Instructions:

1. Beat the Butter:

- In a large bowl, use an electric mixer to beat the softened butter on medium speed until creamy and smooth, about 2-3 minutes.

2. Gradually Add Powdered Sugar:

- Gradually add 3 cups of powdered sugar, one cup at a time, beating on low speed until well combined. Scrape down the sides of the bowl as needed.

3. Add Cream and Vanilla:

- Add the heavy cream (or milk) and vanilla extract. Beat on medium speed until smooth and fluffy. If the frosting is too thick, add more cream or milk, a teaspoon at a time, until you reach the desired consistency. If it's too thin, add more powdered sugar.

4. Adjust Consistency:

- Taste the frosting and add a pinch of salt if desired. Mix well.

5. Frost the Cupcakes:

- Use a piping bag fitted with your favorite tip or a spatula to frost your cooled cupcakes.

Optional Variations:

- **Chocolate Buttercream:** Add 1/2 cup unsweetened cocoa powder to the powdered sugar. You might need to adjust the amount of cream.
- **Cream Cheese Frosting:** Replace 1/2 cup of the butter with 4 ounces of softened cream cheese.
- **Fruit Flavors:** Fold in fruit preserves or purees, but be mindful of the consistency. You might need to adjust the powdered sugar.

Enjoy your beautifully frosted cupcakes!

Tiramisu

Ingredients:

For the Coffee Mixture:

- 1 cup strong brewed coffee, cooled to room temperature
- 1/4 cup coffee liqueur (e.g., Kahlúa) or Marsala wine (optional)
- 1 tablespoon granulated sugar (optional)

For the Mascarpone Mixture:

- 4 large egg yolks
- 1/2 cup granulated sugar
- 1 cup heavy cream
- 8 ounces mascarpone cheese, softened
- 1 teaspoon vanilla extract

For Assembly:

- 24-30 ladyfingers (savoiardi)
- Unsweetened cocoa powder, for dusting
- Dark chocolate shavings or grated chocolate (optional, for garnish)

Instructions:

1. Prepare the Coffee Mixture:

- In a shallow dish, combine the cooled coffee, coffee liqueur (if using), and granulated sugar (if using). Stir until the sugar is dissolved.

2. Prepare the Mascarpone Mixture:

- In a medium bowl, whisk the egg yolks with the granulated sugar until the mixture is pale and slightly thickened.
- In a large bowl, whip the heavy cream until soft peaks form.
- Gently fold the mascarpone cheese and vanilla extract into the egg yolk mixture until smooth.
- Fold the whipped cream into the mascarpone mixture until well combined and smooth.

3. Assemble the Tiramisu:

- Briefly dip each ladyfinger into the coffee mixture, making sure not to soak them. They should be lightly coated but not soggy.
- Arrange a layer of dipped ladyfingers in the bottom of a 9x13-inch baking dish or a similar-sized serving dish.

- Spread half of the mascarpone mixture over the layer of ladyfingers.
- Add another layer of dipped ladyfingers on top of the mascarpone mixture.
- Spread the remaining mascarpone mixture evenly over the second layer of ladyfingers.

4. Chill:

- Cover the dish with plastic wrap and refrigerate for at least 4 hours, preferably overnight, to allow the flavors to meld and the dessert to set.

5. Serve:

- Before serving, dust the top with unsweetened cocoa powder.
- Garnish with dark chocolate shavings or grated chocolate if desired.

Enjoy your classic Tiramisu with its rich, creamy layers and delightful coffee flavor!

Key Lime Pie

Ingredients:

For the Graham Cracker Crust:

- 1 1/2 cups graham cracker crumbs (about 12-14 graham crackers)
- 1/4 cup granulated sugar
- 6 tablespoons unsalted butter, melted

For the Key Lime Filling:

- 1 can (14 ounces) sweetened condensed milk
- 1/2 cup sour cream
- 1/2 cup fresh key lime juice (or regular lime juice)
- 2 large egg yolks
- 1 teaspoon lime zest (optional)

For the Whipped Cream (Optional):

- 1 cup heavy cream
- 2 tablespoons powdered sugar
- 1 teaspoon vanilla extract

Instructions:

1. Prepare the Crust:

- Preheat your oven to 350°F (175°C).
- In a medium bowl, mix the graham cracker crumbs, granulated sugar, and melted butter until the crumbs are evenly coated and resemble wet sand.
- Press the mixture firmly into the bottom and up the sides of a 9-inch pie pan.
- Bake in the preheated oven for 8-10 minutes, or until the crust is lightly golden and set. Let it cool completely before adding the filling.

2. Prepare the Filling:

- In a large bowl, whisk together the sweetened condensed milk, sour cream, lime juice, and egg yolks until smooth and well combined. If using, stir in the lime zest.
- Pour the filling into the cooled graham cracker crust.

3. Bake the Pie:

- Bake in the preheated oven for 10-12 minutes, or until the filling is set and the edges are slightly puffed. The center may still be a bit jiggly.

- Turn off the oven and leave the pie inside with the door slightly ajar for 1 hour to cool gradually.

4. Chill:

- Transfer the pie to the refrigerator and chill for at least 4 hours, or overnight, to fully set and develop the flavors.

5. Prepare the Whipped Cream (Optional):

- In a medium bowl, beat the heavy cream, powdered sugar, and vanilla extract with an electric mixer until soft peaks form.
- Spread or pipe the whipped cream over the chilled pie before serving.

6. Serve:

- Garnish with extra lime zest or lime slices if desired.
- Slice and enjoy your refreshing Key Lime Pie!

This classic dessert combines a sweet and tangy filling with a crunchy crust and creamy topping, perfect for any occasion.

Snickerdoodles

Ingredients:

For the Cookies:

- 1 cup (2 sticks) unsalted butter, softened
- 1 1/2 cups granulated sugar
- 2 large eggs
- 2 3/4 cups all-purpose flour
- 2 teaspoons cream of tartar
- 1/2 teaspoon baking soda
- 1/4 teaspoon baking powder
- 1/4 teaspoon salt

For Rolling:

- 3 tablespoons granulated sugar
- 1 tablespoon ground cinnamon

Instructions:

1. Preheat Oven:

- Preheat your oven to 375°F (190°C). Line baking sheets with parchment paper or silicone baking mats.

2. Cream Butter and Sugar:

- In a large bowl, use an electric mixer to beat the softened butter and granulated sugar together until light and fluffy.

3. Add Eggs:

- Beat in the eggs, one at a time, mixing well after each addition.

4. Mix Dry Ingredients:

- In a separate bowl, whisk together the flour, cream of tartar, baking soda, baking powder, and salt.

5. Combine Ingredients:

- Gradually add the dry ingredients to the wet ingredients, mixing until just combined. Be careful not to overmix.

6. Prepare Cinnamon-Sugar Mixture:

- In a small bowl, combine the 3 tablespoons of granulated sugar with the ground cinnamon.

7. Shape Cookies:

- Scoop about 1 tablespoon of dough and roll it into a ball. Roll the dough balls in the cinnamon-sugar mixture until fully coated.

8. Bake:

- Place the coated dough balls onto the prepared baking sheets, spacing them about 2 inches apart.
- Bake in the preheated oven for 10-12 minutes, or until the edges are lightly golden but the centers are still soft.

9. Cool:

- Allow the cookies to cool on the baking sheets for a few minutes before transferring them to a wire rack to cool completely.

Enjoy your homemade Snickerdoodles with their perfect balance of cinnamon and sweetness!

Pumpkin Pie

Ingredients:

For the Pie Crust:

- 1 1/2 cups all-purpose flour
- 1/4 teaspoon salt
- 1/4 cup granulated sugar
- 1/2 cup (1 stick) unsalted butter, cold and cut into small pieces
- 1/4 cup ice water (more if needed)

For the Pumpkin Filling:

- 1 can (15 ounces) pure pumpkin puree
- 3/4 cup granulated sugar
- 1/2 teaspoon salt
- 1 teaspoon ground cinnamon
- 1/2 teaspoon ground ginger
- 1/4 teaspoon ground cloves
- 2 large eggs
- 1 cup evaporated milk (not sweetened condensed milk)

Instructions:

1. Prepare the Pie Crust:

- In a medium bowl, whisk together the flour, salt, and granulated sugar.
- Cut in the cold butter using a pastry cutter or your fingers until the mixture resembles coarse crumbs.
- Gradually add the ice water, one tablespoon at a time, mixing until the dough comes together. You may need a bit more or less water.
- Shape the dough into a disc, wrap it in plastic wrap, and refrigerate for at least 1 hour.

2. Preheat Oven:

- Preheat your oven to 425°F (220°C).

3. Roll Out the Dough:

- On a lightly floured surface, roll out the chilled dough to fit a 9-inch pie pan. Transfer the dough to the pie pan and trim any excess. Crimp the edges as desired.

4. Blind Bake (Optional but recommended for a crisper crust):

- Line the pie crust with parchment paper or aluminum foil and fill with pie weights or dried beans.
- Bake for 10 minutes, then remove the weights and lining and bake for an additional 5 minutes. Let it cool slightly before adding the filling.

5. Prepare the Pumpkin Filling:

- In a large bowl, whisk together the pumpkin puree, granulated sugar, salt, cinnamon, ginger, and cloves.
- Beat in the eggs until well combined.
- Gradually stir in the evaporated milk until the mixture is smooth.

6. Fill and Bake:

- Pour the pumpkin filling into the partially baked pie crust.
- Bake in the preheated oven at 425°F (220°C) for 15 minutes.
- Reduce the oven temperature to 350°F (175°C) and continue to bake for 35-40 minutes, or until the filling is set and a knife inserted into the center comes out clean. The edges should be lightly browned.

7. Cool:

- Allow the pie to cool completely on a wire rack. The filling will continue to set as it cools.

8. Serve:

- Serve your Pumpkin Pie plain or with a dollop of whipped cream on top.

Enjoy the classic flavors of Pumpkin Pie with its creamy, spiced filling and crisp, buttery crust!

Oatmeal Raisin Cookies

Ingredients:

- 1 cup (2 sticks) unsalted butter, softened
- 1 cup granulated sugar
- 1 cup packed brown sugar
- 2 large eggs
- 1 teaspoon vanilla extract
- 1 1/2 cups all-purpose flour
- 1/2 teaspoon baking soda
- 1/2 teaspoon baking powder
- 1/2 teaspoon salt
- 3 cups old-fashioned rolled oats
- 1 cup raisins
- 1/2 teaspoon ground cinnamon (optional)

Instructions:

1. Preheat Oven:

- Preheat your oven to 350°F (175°C). Line baking sheets with parchment paper or silicone baking mats.

2. Cream Butter and Sugars:

- In a large bowl, use an electric mixer to beat the softened butter, granulated sugar, and brown sugar together until light and fluffy.

3. Add Eggs and Vanilla:

- Beat in the eggs, one at a time, mixing well after each addition. Stir in the vanilla extract.

4. Mix Dry Ingredients:

- In a separate bowl, whisk together the flour, baking soda, baking powder, salt, and ground cinnamon (if using).

5. Combine Ingredients:

- Gradually add the dry ingredients to the wet ingredients, mixing until just combined.
- Stir in the rolled oats and raisins until evenly distributed.

6. Shape Cookies:

- Drop rounded tablespoons of dough onto the prepared baking sheets, spacing them about 2 inches apart.

7. Bake:

- Bake in the preheated oven for 10-12 minutes, or until the edges are golden brown and the centers are set. The cookies will firm up as they cool.

8. Cool:

- Allow the cookies to cool on the baking sheets for a few minutes before transferring them to wire racks to cool completely.

Enjoy your Oatmeal Raisin Cookies with their chewy texture and sweet, comforting flavor!

Peach Cobbler

Ingredients:

For the Peach Filling:

- 6 cups fresh peaches, peeled, pitted, and sliced (about 6-8 medium peaches) or 4 cups canned peaches, drained
- 1 cup granulated sugar
- 1/4 cup cornstarch
- 1/2 teaspoon ground cinnamon
- 1/4 teaspoon ground nutmeg
- 1 tablespoon lemon juice (optional)

For the Topping:

- 1 1/2 cups all-purpose flour
- 1/4 cup granulated sugar
- 1/4 cup packed brown sugar
- 2 teaspoons baking powder
- 1/4 teaspoon salt
- 1/2 cup (1 stick) unsalted butter, cold and cut into small pieces
- 3/4 cup milk

For the Finish:

- 1 tablespoon granulated sugar (for sprinkling on top, optional)

Instructions:

1. Preheat Oven:

- Preheat your oven to 375°F (190°C).

2. Prepare the Peach Filling:

- In a large bowl, combine the sliced peaches with the granulated sugar, cornstarch, cinnamon, nutmeg, and lemon juice (if using). Toss until the peaches are evenly coated.
- Transfer the peach mixture to a 9x13-inch baking dish or a similar-sized ovenproof dish.

3. Prepare the Topping:

- In a medium bowl, whisk together the flour, granulated sugar, brown sugar, baking powder, and salt.
- Cut in the cold butter using a pastry cutter or your fingers until the mixture resembles coarse crumbs.

- Stir in the milk until just combined. The batter will be thick.

4. Assemble the Cobbler:

- Drop spoonfuls of the topping over the peach filling, spreading it out as evenly as possible. It's okay if some of the peach filling is visible.

5. Bake:

- Bake in the preheated oven for 40-45 minutes, or until the topping is golden brown and the peach filling is bubbling. A toothpick inserted into the topping should come out clean.

6. Cool:

- Allow the cobbler to cool slightly before serving. This helps the filling to set a bit.

7. Serve:

- Serve warm, ideally with a scoop of vanilla ice cream or a dollop of whipped cream.

Enjoy the classic taste of Peach Cobbler with its sweet, juicy peaches and buttery topping!

Chocolate Brownie Ice Cream Sundae

Ingredients:

For the Brownies:

- 1/2 cup (1 stick) unsalted butter
- 1 cup granulated sugar
- 2 large eggs
- 1 teaspoon vanilla extract
- 1/3 cup unsweetened cocoa powder
- 1/2 cup all-purpose flour
- 1/4 teaspoon salt
- 1/4 teaspoon baking powder

For the Sundae:

- 1 pint vanilla ice cream (or your favorite flavor)
- 1/2 cup chocolate sauce (store-bought or homemade)
- 1/2 cup whipped cream
- 1/4 cup crushed nuts (e.g., peanuts, walnuts, or almonds)
- Maraschino cherries (for garnish)
- Additional chocolate sauce or caramel sauce (optional)

Instructions:

1. Prepare the Brownies:

a. Preheat Oven:

- Preheat your oven to 350°F (175°C). Grease a 9x9-inch baking pan or line it with parchment paper.

b. Melt Butter:

- In a medium saucepan, melt the butter over low heat. Remove from heat.

c. Mix Ingredients:

- Stir the granulated sugar into the melted butter until well combined.
- Beat in the eggs, one at a time, followed by the vanilla extract.
- Mix in the cocoa powder, flour, salt, and baking powder until just combined.

d. Bake Brownies:

- Pour the brownie batter into the prepared pan and spread it evenly.

- Bake for 20-25 minutes, or until a toothpick inserted into the center comes out mostly clean. The brownies should be set but still fudgy.
- Allow the brownies to cool completely before cutting them into squares.

2. Assemble the Sundae:

a. Scoop Ice Cream:

- Place a scoop of vanilla ice cream into each serving bowl or dish.

b. Add Brownie Pieces:

- Cut the cooled brownies into bite-sized pieces and place them on top of the ice cream.

c. Drizzle with Chocolate Sauce:

- Drizzle chocolate sauce over the brownie and ice cream.

d. Top with Whipped Cream:

- Add a generous dollop of whipped cream on top.

e. Garnish:

- Sprinkle with crushed nuts and top with a maraschino cherry.
- Drizzle with additional chocolate or caramel sauce if desired.

3. Serve:

- Serve the Chocolate Brownie Ice Cream Sundae immediately for the best experience.

Enjoy this indulgent dessert that combines rich chocolate brownies, creamy ice cream, and all your favorite sundae toppings!

Raspberry Jam

Ingredients:

- 4 cups fresh raspberries (about 1 pint or 500 grams)
- 1/4 cup lemon juice (about 2 lemons)
- 1/2 cup water
- 1 package (1.75 ounces or 49 grams) fruit pectin (such as Sure-Jell or Ball)
- 3 cups granulated sugar

Instructions:

1. Prepare Jars:

- Sterilize your canning jars and lids by placing them in a boiling water bath for 10 minutes. Keep them hot until ready to use.

2. Prepare Raspberries:

- In a large pot, combine the raspberries, lemon juice, and water. Mash the raspberries with a potato masher or the back of a spoon to release their juices.

3. Cook Fruit Mixture:

- Over medium heat, bring the mixture to a boil. Stir frequently.

4. Add Pectin:

- Once boiling, stir in the fruit pectin. Continue to boil the mixture for 1-2 minutes, stirring constantly.

5. Add Sugar:

- Gradually add the granulated sugar, stirring well to dissolve. Return the mixture to a rolling boil and cook for 1-2 minutes, or until the jam reaches the desired consistency (use the "gel test" to check if it's set).

6. Test Consistency:

- To test the consistency, place a spoonful of the jam on a cold plate and let it sit for a minute. Run your finger through the jam; if it wrinkles and holds its shape, it's ready. If not, boil for another minute and test again.

7. Fill Jars:

- Carefully pour the hot jam into the prepared, sterilized jars, leaving about 1/4 inch of headspace at the top. Wipe the rims of the jars with a clean, damp cloth to remove any residue.

8. Seal Jars:

- Place the sterilized lids on the jars and screw on the metal bands until fingertip-tight.

9. Process Jars:

- Process the jars in a boiling water bath for 5-10 minutes to ensure they are sealed properly. Adjust the processing time based on your altitude if necessary.

10. Cool and Store:

- Remove the jars from the water bath and let them cool completely on a clean towel or rack. Once cooled, check the seals by pressing down in the center of the lid. If it doesn't pop back, the jar is sealed properly. Store the sealed jars in a cool, dark place.

11. Enjoy:

- Your homemade raspberry jam is now ready to enjoy on toast, in desserts, or as a sweet addition to your favorite recipes!

This simple recipe yields a vibrant and flavorful raspberry jam with a perfect balance of sweetness and tartness.

Coconut Cream Pie

Ingredients:

For the Pie Crust:

- 1 1/2 cups all-purpose flour
- 1/4 teaspoon salt
- 1/4 cup granulated sugar
- 1/2 cup (1 stick) unsalted butter, cold and cut into small pieces
- 1/4 cup ice water (more if needed)

For the Coconut Cream Filling:

- 1 1/2 cups whole milk
- 1 cup coconut milk (from a can, not the kind in the carton)
- 3/4 cup granulated sugar
- 1/4 cup cornstarch
- 1/4 teaspoon salt
- 4 large egg yolks
- 2 tablespoons unsalted butter
- 1 cup shredded sweetened coconut (toasted or untoasted, depending on preference)
- 1 teaspoon vanilla extract

For the Topping:

- 1 cup heavy cream
- 2 tablespoons granulated sugar
- 1 teaspoon vanilla extract
- Additional toasted shredded coconut for garnish (optional)

Instructions:

1. Prepare the Pie Crust:

a. Preheat Oven:

- Preheat your oven to 375°F (190°C).

b. Make the Dough:

- In a medium bowl, whisk together the flour, salt, and granulated sugar.
- Cut in the cold butter using a pastry cutter or your fingers until the mixture resembles coarse crumbs.
- Gradually add the ice water, one tablespoon at a time, mixing until the dough comes together. You may need a bit more or less water.

c. Roll Out the Dough:

- Turn the dough out onto a floured surface and roll it to fit a 9-inch pie pan.
- Transfer the dough to the pie pan, trim any excess, and crimp the edges.

d. Blind Bake:

- Line the crust with parchment paper or aluminum foil and fill with pie weights or dried beans.
- Bake in the preheated oven for 15 minutes.
- Remove the weights and lining, and bake for an additional 5-7 minutes, or until the crust is lightly golden. Allow it to cool completely before filling.

2. Prepare the Coconut Cream Filling:

a. Heat Ingredients:

- In a medium saucepan, whisk together the milk, coconut milk, granulated sugar, cornstarch, and salt. Heat over medium heat, whisking constantly until the mixture starts to thicken and just begins to boil.

b. Temper the Egg Yolks:

- In a separate bowl, lightly whisk the egg yolks. Slowly add a few spoonfuls of the hot milk mixture to the egg yolks while whisking constantly to temper them.

c. Combine and Cook:

- Gradually whisk the tempered egg yolks back into the saucepan with the hot milk mixture. Continue to cook, whisking constantly, until the mixture thickens and comes to a gentle boil.

d. Finish the Filling:

- Remove from heat and stir in the butter, shredded coconut, and vanilla extract until the butter is melted and the mixture is well combined.

e. Cool:

- Pour the filling into the cooled pie crust, smoothing the top with a spatula. Allow it to cool to room temperature, then refrigerate for at least 4 hours, or until fully chilled and set.

3. Prepare the Topping:

a. Whip Cream:

- In a large bowl, beat the heavy cream, granulated sugar, and vanilla extract with an electric mixer until soft peaks form.

b. Spread Cream:

- Spread or pipe the whipped cream over the chilled coconut cream filling.

c. Garnish:

- Garnish with additional toasted shredded coconut if desired.

4. Serve:

- Slice and enjoy your homemade Coconut Cream Pie!

This pie combines a rich and creamy coconut filling with a buttery crust and a light, fluffy topping, making it a delightful dessert for any occasion.

Molasses Cookies

Ingredients:

- 3/4 cup (1 1/2 sticks) unsalted butter, softened
- 1 cup granulated sugar, plus extra for rolling
- 1/2 cup molasses
- 1 large egg
- 2 1/4 cups all-purpose flour
- 2 teaspoons ground ginger
- 1 teaspoon ground cinnamon
- 1/2 teaspoon ground cloves
- 1/2 teaspoon baking soda
- 1/4 teaspoon salt

Instructions:

1. Preheat Oven:

- Preheat your oven to 350°F (175°C). Line baking sheets with parchment paper or silicone baking mats.

2. Cream Butter and Sugar:

- In a large bowl, use an electric mixer to beat the softened butter and 1 cup of granulated sugar together until light and fluffy.

3. Add Molasses and Egg:

- Beat in the molasses and egg until well combined.

4. Mix Dry Ingredients:

- In a separate bowl, whisk together the flour, ground ginger, ground cinnamon, ground cloves, baking soda, and salt.

5. Combine Ingredients:

- Gradually add the dry ingredients to the wet ingredients, mixing until just combined.

6. Shape Cookies:

- Roll the dough into 1-inch balls and roll each ball in granulated sugar to coat. Place the coated dough balls onto the prepared baking sheets, spacing them about 2 inches apart.

7. Bake:

- Bake in the preheated oven for 10-12 minutes, or until the edges are set and the tops are slightly cracked. The centers should be soft but set.

8. Cool:

- Allow the cookies to cool on the baking sheets for a few minutes before transferring them to a wire rack to cool completely.

Enjoy the rich, spicy flavor of these classic Molasses Cookies with a cup of tea or coffee!

Apple Crisp

Ingredients:

For the Apple Filling:

- 6 cups peeled, cored, and sliced apples (about 6 medium apples, such as Granny Smith or Honeycrisp)
- 1/2 cup granulated sugar
- 1/4 cup packed brown sugar
- 1 teaspoon ground cinnamon
- 1/4 teaspoon ground nutmeg
- 1 tablespoon lemon juice
- 2 tablespoons all-purpose flour (to thicken)

For the Crisp Topping:

- 1 cup old-fashioned rolled oats
- 1/2 cup all-purpose flour
- 1/2 cup packed brown sugar
- 1/2 cup (1 stick) unsalted butter, cold and cut into small pieces
- 1/4 teaspoon salt

Instructions:

1. Preheat Oven:

- Preheat your oven to 350°F (175°C). Grease a 9x13-inch baking dish or similar-sized ovenproof dish.

2. Prepare the Apple Filling:

- In a large bowl, combine the sliced apples, granulated sugar, brown sugar, cinnamon, nutmeg, lemon juice, and flour. Toss until the apples are well coated.
- Transfer the apple mixture to the prepared baking dish, spreading it evenly.

3. Prepare the Crisp Topping:

- In a medium bowl, combine the rolled oats, flour, brown sugar, and salt.
- Cut in the cold butter using a pastry cutter or your fingers until the mixture resembles coarse crumbs.

4. Assemble and Bake:

- Sprinkle the crisp topping evenly over the apple filling.

- Bake in the preheated oven for 45-50 minutes, or until the topping is golden brown and the apple filling is bubbly and tender.

5. Cool and Serve:

- Allow the apple crisp to cool slightly before serving. This helps the filling to set a bit.

6. Enjoy:

- Serve warm on its own or with a scoop of vanilla ice cream or a dollop of whipped cream for an extra treat.

This Apple Crisp combines the tartness of apples with a sweet, crunchy topping, making it a comforting dessert perfect for any time of year.

Chocolate Truffles

Ingredients:

For the Truffle Filling:

- 8 ounces (225 grams) semi-sweet or bittersweet chocolate, finely chopped
- 1/2 cup heavy cream
- 2 tablespoons unsalted butter, at room temperature
- 1 teaspoon vanilla extract (optional)

For Coating (choose one or more):

- 1/2 cup cocoa powder (for a classic coating)
- 1/2 cup finely chopped nuts (such as almonds, hazelnuts, or walnuts)
- 1/2 cup shredded coconut
- 1/2 cup powdered sugar
- 1/2 cup melted chocolate (for a chocolate dip)

Instructions:

1. Prepare the Ganache:

a. Heat Cream:

- In a small saucepan, heat the heavy cream over medium heat until it begins to simmer. Do not let it boil.

b. Melt Chocolate:

- Place the chopped chocolate in a heatproof bowl. Pour the hot cream over the chocolate and let it sit for a few minutes to soften.

c. Combine Ingredients:

- Stir the chocolate and cream mixture until smooth and fully combined. Add the butter and vanilla extract (if using), and stir until the butter is melted and incorporated.

d. Chill Ganache:

- Cover the bowl with plastic wrap and refrigerate the ganache for about 1-2 hours, or until it is firm enough to scoop.

2. Shape Truffles:

a. Scoop and Roll:

- Use a small cookie scoop or a spoon to scoop out small portions of the ganache. Roll each portion between your palms to form a smooth ball.

b. Coat Truffles:

- Roll each truffle in your desired coating (cocoa powder, chopped nuts, shredded coconut, or powdered sugar) until fully covered.
- If you are dipping in melted chocolate, dip each truffle into the melted chocolate, allowing any excess to drip off, and then roll in your chosen coating.

3. Chill:

- Place the coated truffles on a baking sheet lined with parchment paper. Refrigerate for about 30 minutes to set the coating.

4. Serve:

- Serve the truffles chilled or at room temperature. Store any leftovers in an airtight container in the refrigerator for up to 2 weeks.

These rich and creamy Chocolate Truffles are perfect for gifting or enjoying as a decadent treat.

Maple Pecan Bars

Ingredients:

For the Crust:

- 1 1/2 cups all-purpose flour
- 1/4 cup granulated sugar
- 1/4 teaspoon salt
- 1/2 cup (1 stick) unsalted butter, cold and cut into small pieces

For the Filling:

- 1 cup pure maple syrup (not pancake syrup)
- 1/2 cup packed brown sugar
- 1/4 cup unsalted butter
- 2 large eggs
- 1 1/2 cups chopped pecans
- 1 teaspoon vanilla extract

Instructions:

1. Preheat Oven:

- Preheat your oven to 350°F (175°C). Grease a 9x9-inch baking pan or line it with parchment paper, leaving an overhang for easy removal.

2. Prepare the Crust:

a. Mix Dry Ingredients:

- In a medium bowl, combine the flour, granulated sugar, and salt.

b. Cut in Butter:

- Cut in the cold butter using a pastry cutter or your fingers until the mixture resembles coarse crumbs.

c. Press into Pan:

- Press the mixture evenly into the bottom of the prepared baking pan to form the crust.

d. Bake Crust:

- Bake in the preheated oven for 15 minutes, or until lightly golden. Remove from the oven and set aside.

3. Prepare the Filling:

a. Heat Ingredients:

- In a medium saucepan, combine the maple syrup, brown sugar, and butter. Cook over medium heat, stirring occasionally, until the mixture is melted and smooth.

b. Cool Slightly:

- Remove from heat and let the mixture cool for about 5 minutes.

c. Add Eggs and Pecans:

- Whisk in the eggs, one at a time, until fully incorporated. Stir in the chopped pecans and vanilla extract.

4. Assemble and Bake:

a. Pour Filling:

- Pour the filling evenly over the pre-baked crust.

b. Bake Bars:

- Return the pan to the oven and bake for 25-30 minutes, or until the filling is set and slightly puffed. A toothpick inserted into the center should come out clean.

5. Cool and Slice:

a. Cool:

- Allow the bars to cool completely in the pan on a wire rack. The filling will set further as it cools.

b. Slice:

- Once cooled, use the parchment paper overhang to lift the bars out of the pan. Cut into squares or bars.

6. Serve:

- Enjoy your Maple Pecan Bars as a sweet treat with a cup of coffee or tea!

These bars combine the rich flavor of maple syrup with crunchy pecans and a buttery crust for a delightful dessert.

Scones

Ingredients:

- 2 cups all-purpose flour
- 1/4 cup granulated sugar
- 1 tablespoon baking powder
- 1/2 teaspoon salt
- 1/2 cup (1 stick) unsalted butter, cold and cut into small pieces
- 2/3 cup milk (whole milk or heavy cream preferred)
- 1 large egg
- 1 teaspoon vanilla extract (optional)

Optional Add-ins:

- 1/2 cup currants, raisins, or dried cranberries
- 1/2 cup chocolate chips
- 1/2 cup chopped nuts
- 1/2 cup fresh or frozen berries (e.g., blueberries, raspberries)

For Brushing:

- 1 tablespoon milk
- 1 tablespoon granulated sugar (for sprinkling, optional)

Instructions:

1. Preheat Oven:

- Preheat your oven to 400°F (200°C). Line a baking sheet with parchment paper or a silicone baking mat.

2. Prepare Dry Ingredients:

- In a large bowl, whisk together the flour, sugar, baking powder, and salt.

3. Cut in Butter:

- Add the cold butter pieces to the flour mixture. Using a pastry cutter, two forks, or your fingers, cut the butter into the flour until the mixture resembles coarse crumbs with some pea-sized pieces of butter remaining.

4. Mix Wet Ingredients:

- In a separate bowl, whisk together the milk, egg, and vanilla extract (if using).

5. Combine Ingredients:

- Pour the wet ingredients into the dry ingredients and stir gently until just combined. If you're adding any optional mix-ins (e.g., currants, chocolate chips, or berries), fold them in at this stage.

6. Shape and Cut:

- Turn the dough out onto a lightly floured surface. Gently knead the dough a few times to bring it together. Pat it into a 1-inch thick circle.
- Using a knife or a round biscuit cutter, cut the dough into 8 wedges or rounds. Place the scones on the prepared baking sheet.

7. Brush and Sprinkle (Optional):

- Brush the tops of the scones with milk and sprinkle with granulated sugar, if desired.

8. Bake:

- Bake in the preheated oven for 15-20 minutes, or until the scones are golden brown on top and cooked through.

9. Cool:

- Allow the scones to cool slightly on a wire rack before serving.

10. Serve:

- Enjoy the scones warm or at room temperature, with butter, jam, or clotted cream.

These scones are versatile and can be customized with your favorite add-ins or enjoyed plain. They're perfect for breakfast, brunch, or as a delightful snack!

French Toast

Ingredients:

- 4 large eggs
- 1 cup milk (whole milk or 2% preferred)
- 1 teaspoon vanilla extract
- 1 teaspoon ground cinnamon (optional)
- 1/4 teaspoon salt
- 8 slices of bread (thick slices like brioche, challah, or Texas toast work best)
- 2 tablespoons unsalted butter (for cooking)

Optional Toppings:

- Maple syrup
- Fresh berries
- Powdered sugar
- Whipped cream
- Sliced bananas
- Nutella or jam

Instructions:

1. Prepare the Batter:

- In a large bowl, whisk together the eggs, milk, vanilla extract, ground cinnamon (if using), and salt until well combined.

2. Heat the Pan:

- Heat a large skillet or griddle over medium heat. Add 1 tablespoon of butter and let it melt, coating the pan evenly.

3. Dip the Bread:

- Dip each slice of bread into the egg mixture, allowing it to soak for a few seconds on each side. Let the excess batter drip off before placing it in the pan.

4. Cook the French Toast:

- Place the soaked bread slices in the hot skillet or griddle. Cook for 2-3 minutes on each side, or until golden brown and slightly crispy. Add more butter to the pan as needed.

5. Keep Warm:

- Transfer the cooked French toast to a plate and keep warm in a low oven (around 200°F or 95°C) while you cook the remaining slices.

6. Serve:

- Serve the French toast warm with your choice of toppings. Drizzle with maple syrup, sprinkle with powdered sugar, and add fresh berries or sliced bananas as desired.

Enjoy your homemade French Toast as a delightful and satisfying breakfast!

Bread Pudding

Ingredients:

For the Bread Pudding:

- 6 cups stale bread, cut into 1-inch cubes (preferably a crusty bread like French or Italian)
- 4 large eggs
- 2 cups whole milk
- 1 cup heavy cream
- 1 cup granulated sugar
- 1 tablespoon vanilla extract
- 1 teaspoon ground cinnamon
- 1/2 teaspoon ground nutmeg
- 1/4 teaspoon salt
- 1/2 cup raisins or currants (optional)

For the Sauce (optional):

- 1/2 cup butter
- 1 cup powdered sugar
- 1/4 cup milk
- 1 teaspoon vanilla extract

Instructions:

1. Preheat Oven:

- Preheat your oven to 350°F (175°C). Grease a 9x13-inch baking dish or similar-sized ovenproof dish.

2. Prepare the Bread:

- Spread the bread cubes evenly in the prepared baking dish.

3. Make the Custard:

- In a large bowl, whisk together the eggs, milk, heavy cream, granulated sugar, vanilla extract, ground cinnamon, ground nutmeg, and salt until well combined.

4. Combine Bread and Custard:

- Pour the custard mixture evenly over the bread cubes. Gently press the bread cubes down with a spatula to ensure they are fully soaked with the custard mixture. If using raisins or currants, sprinkle them over the top.

5. Bake:

- Bake in the preheated oven for 45-50 minutes, or until the pudding is set in the center and the top is golden brown. A knife inserted into the center should come out clean.

6. Prepare the Sauce (optional):

- While the bread pudding is baking, you can make the sauce. In a small saucepan, melt the butter over medium heat. Whisk in the powdered sugar and milk until smooth and well combined. Remove from heat and stir in the vanilla extract.

7. Cool and Serve:

- Allow the bread pudding to cool slightly before serving. Drizzle with the optional sauce, if desired.

8. Enjoy:

- Serve warm or at room temperature, optionally with a scoop of vanilla ice cream or a dollop of whipped cream.

This Bread Pudding is a comforting and versatile dessert that can be customized with various add-ins or toppings. It's perfect for using up leftover bread and can be enjoyed as a delicious treat any time of year.

Mousse

Ingredients:

- 6 ounces (170 grams) semi-sweet or bittersweet chocolate, chopped
- 2 tablespoons unsalted butter
- 3 large eggs, separated
- 1/4 cup granulated sugar
- 1/2 cup heavy cream
- 1/2 teaspoon vanilla extract (optional)
- Pinch of salt

Optional Garnishes:

- Whipped cream
- Shaved chocolate
- Fresh berries
- Mint leaves

Instructions:

1. Melt the Chocolate:

- In a heatproof bowl, combine the chopped chocolate and butter. Melt over a double boiler or in the microwave in 20-second intervals, stirring until smooth. Let the melted chocolate cool slightly.

2. Prepare the Egg Yolks:

- In a medium bowl, whisk the egg yolks with the granulated sugar until the mixture is pale and slightly thickened. Gently fold in the melted chocolate mixture until fully combined. Stir in the vanilla extract if using.

3. Whip the Egg Whites:

- In a separate clean, dry bowl, beat the egg whites with a pinch of salt until stiff peaks form. Gently fold the whipped egg whites into the chocolate mixture in thirds, being careful not to deflate the mixture.

4. Whip the Cream:

- In another bowl, whip the heavy cream until soft peaks form. Fold the whipped cream into the chocolate mixture until well combined and smooth.

5. Chill:

- Spoon the mousse into individual serving dishes or glasses. Refrigerate for at least 2 hours, or until set.

6. Garnish and Serve:

- Just before serving, garnish with whipped cream, shaved chocolate, fresh berries, or mint leaves, if desired.

7. Enjoy:

- Serve chilled and enjoy the rich, creamy texture of this classic chocolate mousse!

This chocolate mousse is a luxurious and versatile dessert that can be customized with different flavors or garnishes according to your preference.

Whoopie Pies

For the Cake:

- 2 1/2 cups all-purpose flour
- 1 1/2 teaspoons baking powder
- 1 teaspoon baking soda
- 1/2 teaspoon salt
- 1 cup unsalted butter, at room temperature
- 1 cup granulated sugar
- 1 cup packed brown sugar
- 2 large eggs
- 1 cup milk
- 1 teaspoon vanilla extract
- 1 cup unsweetened cocoa powder (for chocolate whoopie pies) or omit for vanilla whoopie pies

For the Filling:

- 1/2 cup unsalted butter, at room temperature
- 1 1/2 cups powdered sugar
- 1/4 cup heavy cream
- 1 teaspoon vanilla extract

Instructions:

1. Preheat Oven:

- Preheat your oven to 375°F (190°C). Line baking sheets with parchment paper or silicone baking mats.

2. Prepare the Cake Batter:

a. Mix Dry Ingredients:

- In a medium bowl, whisk together the flour, baking powder, baking soda, salt, and cocoa powder (if using).

b. Cream Butter and Sugars:

- In a large bowl, beat the butter, granulated sugar, and brown sugar together until light and fluffy.

c. Add Eggs and Vanilla:

- Beat in the eggs one at a time, followed by the vanilla extract.

d. Combine Dry and Wet Ingredients:

- Gradually add the dry ingredients to the butter mixture, alternating with the milk. Mix until just combined.

3. Scoop and Bake:

a. Scoop Batter:

- Drop rounded tablespoons of batter onto the prepared baking sheets, spacing them about 2 inches apart. Use a cookie scoop or spoon for uniform sizes.

b. Bake:

- Bake in the preheated oven for 10-12 minutes, or until the cakes are set and a toothpick inserted into the center comes out clean.

c. Cool:

- Allow the cakes to cool on the baking sheets for a few minutes before transferring them to a wire rack to cool completely.

4. Prepare the Filling:

a. Beat Ingredients:

- In a medium bowl, beat the butter until creamy. Gradually add the powdered sugar and continue to beat until smooth.

b. Add Cream and Vanilla:

- Mix in the heavy cream and vanilla extract until the filling is light and fluffy.

5. Assemble the Whoopie Pies:

a. Match Cake Sizes:

- Pair the cooled cakes into matching sizes.

b. Fill and Sandwich:

- Spread or pipe the filling onto the flat side of one cake, then top with another cake, flat side down.

6. Serve:

- Enjoy immediately or store in an airtight container for up to 3 days.

These Whoopie Pies are versatile, and you can experiment with different flavors of cake and filling to suit your tastes. Enjoy your homemade treat!

Almond Cake

Ingredients:

For the Cake:

- 1 cup almond flour (also known as almond meal)
- 1 cup all-purpose flour
- 1 cup granulated sugar
- 1/2 cup unsalted butter, at room temperature
- 4 large eggs
- 1 teaspoon vanilla extract
- 1 teaspoon almond extract
- 1/2 cup milk
- 1 1/2 teaspoons baking powder
- 1/4 teaspoon salt

For the Glaze (optional):

- 1/2 cup powdered sugar
- 1-2 tablespoons milk or almond milk
- 1/2 teaspoon almond extract

For Garnish (optional):

- Sliced almonds
- Fresh berries
- Powdered sugar

Instructions:

1. Preheat Oven:

- Preheat your oven to 350°F (175°C). Grease and flour an 8-inch round cake pan or line it with parchment paper.

2. Prepare the Cake Batter:

a. Mix Dry Ingredients:

- In a medium bowl, whisk together the almond flour, all-purpose flour, baking powder, and salt.

b. Cream Butter and Sugar:

- In a large bowl, beat the butter and granulated sugar together until light and fluffy.

c. Add Eggs and Extracts:

- Beat in the eggs one at a time, mixing well after each addition. Then, add the vanilla extract and almond extract.

d. Combine Dry and Wet Ingredients:

- Gradually add the dry ingredients to the butter mixture, alternating with the milk, and mix until just combined. Be careful not to overmix.

3. Bake the Cake:

a. Pour Batter:

- Pour the batter into the prepared cake pan and smooth the top with a spatula.

b. Bake:

- Bake in the preheated oven for 25-30 minutes, or until a toothpick inserted into the center comes out clean and the cake is golden brown.

c. Cool:

- Allow the cake to cool in the pan for about 10 minutes before transferring it to a wire rack to cool completely.

4. Prepare the Glaze (optional):

a. Mix Glaze Ingredients:

- In a small bowl, whisk together the powdered sugar, milk (or almond milk), and almond extract until smooth. Adjust the consistency by adding more milk or powdered sugar as needed.

5. Glaze and Garnish (optional):

a. Glaze the Cake:

- Drizzle the glaze over the cooled cake, allowing it to drip down the sides.

b. Add Garnishes:

- Garnish with sliced almonds, fresh berries, or a dusting of powdered sugar, if desired.

6. Serve:

- Slice and serve the Almond Cake as a delightful treat with tea or coffee.

This Almond Cake is moist and flavorful, with a lovely almond aroma and taste. It's perfect for any occasion or simply as a special dessert for yourself. Enjoy!

Sweet Rolls

Ingredients:

For the Dough:

- 2 ¼ teaspoons active dry yeast (1 packet)
- 1 cup warm milk (110°F)
- ¼ cup granulated sugar
- ¼ cup unsalted butter, melted
- 1 large egg
- 4 cups all-purpose flour
- ½ teaspoon salt

For the Filling:

- ¾ cup packed brown sugar
- 2 tablespoons ground cinnamon
- ¼ cup unsalted butter, softened

For the Cream Cheese Frosting:

- 4 oz cream cheese, softened
- 2 tablespoons unsalted butter, softened
- 1 cup powdered sugar
- 1 teaspoon vanilla extract

Instructions:

1. **Prepare the Dough:**
    - In a small bowl, combine the warm milk and sugar. Sprinkle the yeast on top and let it sit for about 5 minutes, or until the mixture is frothy.
    - In a large mixing bowl, combine the melted butter and egg. Add the yeast mixture and stir to combine.
    - Gradually add the flour and salt, mixing until the dough comes together. Turn the dough onto a lightly floured surface and knead for about 5-7 minutes, or until smooth and elastic.
    - Place the dough in a greased bowl, cover with a clean cloth, and let it rise in a warm, draft-free place for about 1-2 hours, or until doubled in size.
2. **Prepare the Filling:**
    - In a medium bowl, mix the brown sugar and cinnamon.
3. **Assemble the Rolls:**
    - Punch down the dough and turn it onto a floured surface. Roll out into a rectangle approximately 12x16 inches.
    - Spread the softened butter evenly over the dough. Sprinkle the cinnamon-sugar mixture over the butter.

- Starting at the long edge, roll the dough up tightly into a log. Slice into 12 even pieces.
4. **Bake:**
    - Arrange the rolls in a greased 9x13-inch baking pan or two 9-inch round pans. Cover with a cloth and let rise for about 30-45 minutes, or until puffy.
    - Preheat your oven to 375°F (190°C). Bake for 20-25 minutes, or until golden brown.
5. **Prepare the Frosting:**
    - In a medium bowl, beat the cream cheese and butter until smooth. Gradually add the powdered sugar and vanilla extract, beating until creamy.
6. **Finish:**
    - Spread the frosting over the warm rolls.

These cinnamon rolls are sure to be a hit whether you're making them for breakfast or a special treat!

Raspberry Lemon Bars

Ingredients:

For the Crust:

- 1 ¾ cups all-purpose flour
- ⅓ cup granulated sugar
- ½ teaspoon salt
- ½ cup unsalted butter, cold and cut into small pieces

For the Filling:

- 1 cup granulated sugar
- 2 large eggs
- ⅓ cup fresh lemon juice (about 2 lemons)
- 1 tablespoon lemon zest (from 1 lemon)
- 2 tablespoons all-purpose flour
- ½ teaspoon baking powder
- ½ cup fresh or frozen raspberries (thawed and gently patted dry)

For the Topping:

- Powdered sugar, for dusting (optional)

Instructions:

1. **Prepare the Crust:**
   - Preheat your oven to 350°F (175°C). Line an 8x8-inch baking pan with parchment paper, leaving a bit of an overhang for easy removal.
   - In a medium bowl, combine the flour, sugar, and salt. Cut in the cold butter using a pastry cutter or your fingers until the mixture resembles coarse crumbs.
   - Press the mixture evenly into the bottom of the prepared pan. Bake for about 15 minutes, or until lightly golden.
2. **Prepare the Filling:**
   - In a medium bowl, whisk together the sugar and eggs until smooth. Add the lemon juice, lemon zest, flour, and baking powder, and mix until well combined.
   - Gently fold in the raspberries, being careful not to break them up too much.
3. **Assemble and Bake:**
   - Pour the filling over the partially baked crust and spread it out evenly.
   - Bake for 25-30 minutes, or until the filling is set and the edges are slightly golden. A toothpick inserted into the center should come out mostly clean (a few moist crumbs are fine).
4. **Cool and Serve:**
   - Allow the bars to cool completely in the pan on a wire rack.

- Once cool, lift the bars out of the pan using the parchment overhang. Cut into squares.
- Dust with powdered sugar before serving, if desired.

These raspberry lemon bars are perfect for a summer treat or as a light dessert for any occasion. Enjoy!

Chocolate Eclairs

Ingredients:

For the Choux Pastry:

- 1 cup water
- ½ cup unsalted butter
- 1 cup all-purpose flour
- ¼ teaspoon salt
- 4 large eggs

For the Pastry Cream Filling:

- 2 cups whole milk
- ½ cup granulated sugar
- ¼ cup cornstarch
- 4 large egg yolks
- 2 tablespoons unsalted butter
- 1 teaspoon vanilla extract

For the Chocolate Glaze:

- 4 oz semisweet chocolate, chopped
- ¼ cup heavy cream
- 1 tablespoon light corn syrup (optional, for shine)

Instructions:

1. **Prepare the Choux Pastry:**
    - Preheat your oven to 425°F (220°C). Line a baking sheet with parchment paper.
    - In a medium saucepan, bring the water and butter to a boil over medium heat, stirring occasionally.
    - Once boiling, remove from heat and quickly stir in the flour and salt until the mixture forms a smooth ball and pulls away from the sides of the pan.
    - Let the dough cool slightly, then add the eggs one at a time, beating well after each addition until the dough is smooth and glossy.
    - Transfer the dough to a piping bag fitted with a large round or star tip. Pipe 4-5 inch long strips onto the prepared baking sheet, spacing them about 2 inches apart.
    - Bake for 10 minutes at 425°F (220°C), then reduce the temperature to 375°F (190°C) and bake for an additional 20-25 minutes, or until the eclairs are golden brown and crisp. Avoid opening the oven door during baking.
    - Let the eclairs cool completely on a wire rack.
2. **Prepare the Pastry Cream Filling:**
    - In a medium saucepan, heat the milk until it just begins to simmer.

- In a separate bowl, whisk together the sugar, cornstarch, and egg yolks until smooth and pale.
- Gradually whisk the hot milk into the egg mixture to temper it, then return the mixture to the saucepan.
- Cook over medium heat, whisking constantly, until the mixture thickens and begins to boil. Continue to cook for an additional 1-2 minutes.
- Remove from heat and whisk in the butter and vanilla extract. Transfer the pastry cream to a bowl, cover with plastic wrap (pressing the wrap directly onto the surface of the cream to prevent a skin from forming), and let it cool to room temperature.

3. **Prepare the Chocolate Glaze:**
   - In a small saucepan, heat the cream over medium heat until it begins to simmer.
   - Pour the hot cream over the chopped chocolate in a heatproof bowl. Let it sit for 1-2 minutes, then stir until smooth. If using, stir in the corn syrup for added shine.
   - Let the glaze cool slightly before using.

4. **Assemble the Eclairs:**
   - Once the eclairs are completely cool, use a sharp knife to make a small slit in the side of each one.
   - Transfer the pastry cream to a piping bag fitted with a small round tip and fill each eclair through the slit.
   - Dip the top of each filled eclair into the chocolate glaze or spoon the glaze over the top. Allow the glaze to set before serving.

Enjoy your homemade chocolate eclairs! They're a delicious treat for special occasions or just because.

Panna Cotta

Ingredients:

For the Panna Cotta:

- 1 cup whole milk
- 1 cup heavy cream
- ½ cup granulated sugar
- 1 teaspoon vanilla extract (or 1 vanilla bean, split and scraped)
- 2 ½ teaspoons (1 packet) unflavored gelatin
- 3 tablespoons water (for blooming gelatin)

For the Berry Compote:

- 1 cup mixed berries (such as raspberries, blueberries, and strawberries)
- ¼ cup granulated sugar
- 1 tablespoon lemon juice

Instructions:

1. **Prepare the Panna Cotta:**
   - **Bloom the Gelatin:** In a small bowl, sprinkle the gelatin over the water and let it sit for about 5 minutes to bloom.
   - **Heat the Cream and Milk:** In a medium saucepan, combine the milk, cream, and sugar. If using a vanilla bean, add the bean and seeds to the mixture. Heat over medium heat until the sugar dissolves and the mixture is hot but not boiling.
   - **Add the Gelatin:** Remove the pan from the heat. Stir in the bloomed gelatin until fully dissolved. If using vanilla extract, add it now. (If using vanilla bean, remove it from the pan.)
   - **Cool and Set:** Pour the mixture into individual serving glasses or ramekins. Allow to cool to room temperature, then cover and refrigerate for at least 4 hours, or until set.
2. **Prepare the Berry Compote:**
   - In a medium saucepan, combine the berries, sugar, and lemon juice. Cook over medium heat, stirring occasionally, until the berries break down and the mixture thickens slightly, about 10 minutes.
   - Remove from heat and let cool to room temperature. You can also refrigerate the compote if you prefer it chilled.
3. **Serve:**
   - Once the panna cotta is set, spoon the berry compote over the top of each serving.
   - Garnish with additional fresh berries or a mint leaf if desired.

Tips:

- **Flavor Variations:** You can infuse the cream with different flavors such as coffee, citrus zest, or herbs. Just heat the cream with the flavoring ingredients and strain them out before adding the gelatin.
- **For a Healthier Option:** Substitute some of the heavy cream with more milk or use a non-dairy milk alternative, though the texture might be slightly different.

Panna cotta is wonderfully versatile and can be adapted to suit many different tastes. Enjoy!

Chocolate Fondue

Ingredients:

- 8 oz (about 225 grams) semi-sweet or dark chocolate, chopped
- 1 cup heavy cream
- 2 tablespoons unsalted butter
- 1 teaspoon vanilla extract (optional)
- Pinch of salt (optional)

Dippables:

- Fresh fruits (e.g., strawberries, bananas, apples, pears)
- Marshmallows
- Cubes of pound cake or sponge cake
- Pretzels
- Biscotti
- Cube of pound cake or brownie

Instructions:

1. **Prepare the Chocolate:**
   - Chop the chocolate into small, uniform pieces. This helps it melt evenly.
2. **Heat the Cream:**
   - In a medium saucepan, heat the heavy cream over medium heat until it just begins to simmer. Do not let it boil.
3. **Combine Chocolate and Cream:**
   - Remove the pan from heat. Add the chopped chocolate to the hot cream and let it sit for 1-2 minutes to soften.
   - Stir the mixture until smooth and glossy. If using, stir in the vanilla extract and a pinch of salt.
4. **Add Butter (Optional):**
   - For extra richness and smoothness, stir in the unsalted butter until fully incorporated.
5. **Transfer to Fondue Pot:**
   - Pour the chocolate mixture into a fondue pot or a heatproof bowl. If using a fondue pot with a flame or electric heater, keep the chocolate warm and melted.
6. **Serve with Dippables:**
   - Arrange your dippables on a platter around the fondue pot. Provide skewers or forks for dipping.

Tips:

- **Chocolate Choices:** You can use milk chocolate, dark chocolate, or a mix of both, depending on your preference.

- **Keep Warm:** If the chocolate starts to cool and thicken, gently reheat it over a low flame or in the microwave in short bursts, stirring between each burst.
- **Flavor Variations:** Add liqueurs (like Grand Marnier or Kahlua) or flavored extracts (like almond or peppermint) for different flavor profiles.
- **Smoothness:** If the fondue becomes too thick, you can thin it out with a bit more warm cream.

Chocolate fondue is a versatile treat that can be enjoyed with a wide variety of foods. It's always a hit at gatherings and adds a touch of indulgence to any occasion. Enjoy your fondue experience!

Granola Bars

Ingredients:

- 2 cups old-fashioned oats
- 1 cup nuts (e.g., almonds, walnuts, cashews), chopped
- ½ cup seeds (e.g., sunflower seeds, pumpkin seeds)
- ½ cup dried fruit (e.g., cranberries, raisins, apricots), chopped if large
- ¼ cup honey or maple syrup
- ¼ cup unsweetened nut butter (e.g., almond butter, peanut butter)
- ¼ cup brown sugar (optional, for added sweetness)
- 1 teaspoon vanilla extract
- A pinch of salt

Instructions:

1. **Preheat Oven and Prepare Pan:**
    - Preheat your oven to 350°F (175°C). Line an 8x8-inch baking pan with parchment paper, leaving an overhang for easy removal.
2. **Toast the Oats and Nuts:**
    - Spread the oats and chopped nuts on a baking sheet. Toast in the preheated oven for about 8-10 minutes, stirring once, until lightly golden. This step is optional but adds extra flavor and crunch.
3. **Prepare the Wet Ingredients:**
    - In a medium saucepan, combine the honey (or maple syrup), nut butter, and brown sugar (if using). Heat over medium heat, stirring until the mixture is smooth and the sugar is dissolved. Remove from heat and stir in the vanilla extract and salt.
4. **Combine Ingredients:**
    - In a large bowl, mix the toasted oats, nuts, seeds, and dried fruit.
    - Pour the wet mixture over the dry ingredients and stir until everything is evenly coated.
5. **Press and Set:**
    - Transfer the mixture to the prepared baking pan. Use the back of a spoon or your hands (dampened to prevent sticking) to press the mixture firmly and evenly into the pan.
    - Refrigerate for at least 2 hours, or until set. For quicker results, you can also freeze them for about 30 minutes.
6. **Cut and Store:**
    - Once set, lift the granola slab out of the pan using the parchment paper and cut into bars or squares.
    - Store in an airtight container at room temperature for up to a week or in the refrigerator for up to 2 weeks. You can also freeze them for longer storage.

Variations and Tips:

- **Flavor Add-Ins:** Add spices like cinnamon or nutmeg to the dry ingredients for extra flavor.
- **Chocolate:** Mix in some mini chocolate chips or drizzle melted chocolate over the bars before chilling.
- **Coconut:** Add shredded coconut for a tropical twist.
- **Protein:** Boost the protein content by adding a scoop of protein powder to the mixture.

These granola bars are perfect for breakfast on the go, a mid-day snack, or even a post-workout boost. Enjoy!

Lemon Glaze

Ingredients:

- 1 cup powdered sugar
- 2 tablespoons fresh lemon juice
- 1 teaspoon lemon zest (optional, for extra flavor)
- 1-2 tablespoons milk or water (if needed, to adjust consistency)

Instructions:

1. **Mix Ingredients:**
   - In a medium bowl, sift the powdered sugar to remove any lumps.
   - Add the lemon juice and lemon zest (if using) to the powdered sugar.
   - Stir until smooth. If the glaze is too thick, add a small amount of milk or water, a teaspoon at a time, until you reach the desired consistency. It should be pourable but still thick enough to coat your baked goods.
2. **Apply the Glaze:**
   - Drizzle or spread the glaze over your cooled baked goods using a spoon or spatula.
   - Let the glaze set before serving or storing. This usually takes about 15-30 minutes, depending on the thickness of the glaze.

Tips and Variations:

- **Consistency:** Adjust the glaze consistency based on your preference. For a thicker glaze, use less liquid. For a thinner glaze, add more liquid.
- **Flavor Variations:** Experiment with other citrus juices like lime or orange for different flavors. You can also add a bit of vanilla extract or almond extract for a subtle flavor twist.
- **Color:** For a vibrant color, you can add a few drops of food coloring, especially if you want to match a theme or occasion.

Uses:

- **Cakes:** Drizzle over bundt cakes, pound cakes, or sheet cakes.
- **Muffins and Scones:** Pour over muffins or scones for a sweet finish.
- **Cookies:** Use as a topping for sugar cookies or shortbread.

This lemon glaze is versatile and enhances the flavor of many baked treats with its bright and tangy sweetness. Enjoy!

Coffee Cake

Ingredients:

For the Cake:

- 2 ½ cups all-purpose flour
- 1 ½ teaspoons baking powder
- ½ teaspoon baking soda
- ½ teaspoon salt
- ½ cup unsalted butter, softened
- 1 cup granulated sugar
- 2 large eggs
- 1 cup sour cream or plain Greek yogurt
- 1 teaspoon vanilla extract

For the Streusel Topping:

- ¾ cup all-purpose flour
- ½ cup packed brown sugar
- 1 teaspoon ground cinnamon
- ¼ teaspoon salt
- ¼ cup unsalted butter, cold and cut into small pieces

Instructions:

1. **Preheat Oven and Prepare Pan:**
    - Preheat your oven to 350°F (175°C). Grease and flour a 9x13-inch baking pan or line it with parchment paper.
2. **Make the Streusel Topping:**
    - In a medium bowl, combine the flour, brown sugar, cinnamon, and salt. Cut in the cold butter using a pastry cutter or your fingers until the mixture resembles coarse crumbs. Set aside.
3. **Prepare the Cake Batter:**
    - In a medium bowl, whisk together the flour, baking powder, baking soda, and salt.
    - In a large bowl, cream together the softened butter and granulated sugar until light and fluffy.
    - Add the eggs one at a time, beating well after each addition.
    - Mix in the vanilla extract.
    - Gradually add the dry ingredients to the butter mixture, alternating with the sour cream or yogurt, beginning and ending with the dry ingredients. Mix until just combined.
4. **Assemble the Cake:**
    - Spread half of the batter evenly in the prepared baking pan.
    - Sprinkle about half of the streusel topping over the batter.

- Spread the remaining batter over the streusel layer and then sprinkle the remaining streusel topping on top.
5. **Bake:**
   - Bake in the preheated oven for 35-45 minutes, or until a toothpick inserted into the center comes out clean and the top is golden brown.
6. **Cool and Serve:**
   - Allow the coffee cake to cool in the pan for about 10 minutes before transferring to a wire rack to cool completely.
   - Serve warm or at room temperature.

Tips and Variations:

- **Add-ins:** You can add nuts (like walnuts or pecans) or dried fruits (like raisins or cranberries) to the streusel topping or the cake batter for extra texture and flavor.
- **Flavor Variations:** Swap out the cinnamon for other spices like nutmeg or cardamom. You can also add a splash of almond extract or citrus zest for a different twist.
- **Glaze:** For extra sweetness, drizzle a simple glaze (made from powdered sugar and a little milk) over the cooled coffee cake.

This coffee cake is perfect for breakfast, brunch, or as an afternoon snack. Enjoy!

Strawberry Rhubarb Pie

Ingredients:

For the Pie Crust (Makes one double-crust pie):

- 2 ½ cups all-purpose flour
- 1 teaspoon granulated sugar
- 1 teaspoon salt
- 1 cup (2 sticks) unsalted butter, cold and cut into small cubes
- 6-8 tablespoons ice water

For the Filling:

- 2 cups fresh strawberries, hulled and sliced
- 2 cups fresh rhubarb, cut into ½-inch pieces
- 1 cup granulated sugar
- ¼ cup cornstarch
- ¼ teaspoon salt
- 1 tablespoon lemon juice
- 1 teaspoon vanilla extract (optional)

Instructions:

1. **Prepare the Pie Crust:**
    - In a large bowl, whisk together the flour, sugar, and salt.
    - Add the cold butter cubes and use a pastry cutter or your fingers to work the butter into the flour until the mixture resembles coarse crumbs with pea-sized pieces of butter.
    - Gradually add ice water, 1 tablespoon at a time, mixing until the dough just comes together. You may not need all the water.
    - Divide the dough into two equal parts, shape each into a disk, wrap in plastic wrap, and refrigerate for at least 1 hour.
2. **Prepare the Filling:**
    - In a large bowl, combine the strawberries, rhubarb, sugar, cornstarch, salt, lemon juice, and vanilla extract (if using). Toss until the fruit is well-coated. Set aside.
3. **Assemble the Pie:**
    - Preheat your oven to 425°F (220°C).
    - On a lightly floured surface, roll out one disk of dough to fit a 9-inch pie plate. Carefully transfer the rolled-out dough to the pie plate and trim the edges, leaving a slight overhang.
    - Spoon the fruit filling into the crust, spreading it evenly.
    - Roll out the second disk of dough and place it over the filling. Trim and crimp the edges to seal the pie. You can also create a lattice top by cutting the second disk into strips and arranging them over the filling in a crisscross pattern.

- Cut a few slits in the top crust (if using a full crust) to allow steam to escape. Brush the top with a bit of milk or cream and sprinkle with sugar for a golden, crispy finish.
4. **Bake the Pie:**
    - Place the pie on a baking sheet to catch any drips. Bake in the preheated oven for 45-55 minutes, or until the crust is golden brown and the filling is bubbly.
    - If the edges of the crust brown too quickly, cover them with foil or a pie shield.
5. **Cool and Serve:**
    - Allow the pie to cool completely on a wire rack before slicing. This helps the filling set and makes it easier to cut clean slices.

Tips and Variations:

- **Sweetness Level:** Adjust the amount of sugar in the filling based on the sweetness of your strawberries and rhubarb.
- **Spices:** Add a pinch of cinnamon or nutmeg to the filling for additional flavor.
- **Crust:** Use a pre-made pie crust for convenience, or try a graham cracker crust for a different texture.

This strawberry rhubarb pie is a perfect dessert for spring and summer, bringing together a harmonious blend of sweet and tart flavors. Enjoy!

Chocolate Soufflé

Ingredients:

- 2 tablespoons unsalted butter (for greasing ramekins)
- ¼ cup granulated sugar (for coating ramekins)
- 6 oz (170 grams) semisweet or bittersweet chocolate, chopped
- 2 tablespoons unsalted butter
- 3 large eggs, separated
- ¼ cup granulated sugar
- 1 teaspoon vanilla extract
- A pinch of salt

Instructions:

1. **Prepare Ramekins:**
   - Preheat your oven to 375°F (190°C).
   - Generously butter 4 ramekins (6-ounce size) and sprinkle the inside with granulated sugar, tapping out any excess. This helps the soufflé rise evenly.
2. **Melt Chocolate:**
   - In a heatproof bowl set over a pot of simmering water (double boiler method), melt the chopped chocolate and 2 tablespoons of butter together, stirring until smooth. Alternatively, you can melt them in the microwave in 30-second intervals, stirring between each interval.
   - Once melted and smooth, remove from heat and let it cool slightly.
3. **Prepare the Soufflé Base:**
   - In a large bowl, whisk the egg yolks until they are pale and slightly thickened. Stir in the melted chocolate mixture and vanilla extract until well combined.
4. **Beat Egg Whites:**
   - In a clean, dry bowl, use an electric mixer to beat the egg whites and a pinch of salt until soft peaks form.
   - Gradually add the ¼ cup granulated sugar and continue to beat until stiff, glossy peaks form.
5. **Fold Egg Whites into Chocolate Mixture:**
   - Gently fold one-third of the beaten egg whites into the chocolate mixture to lighten it.
   - Carefully fold in the remaining egg whites in two additions, making sure not to deflate the mixture. Be gentle and use a folding motion to retain the airiness.
6. **Fill Ramekins:**
   - Divide the soufflé mixture evenly among the prepared ramekins. Run your thumb around the edge of each ramekin to help the soufflés rise evenly.
7. **Bake:**
   - Place the ramekins on a baking sheet and bake in the preheated oven for 12-15 minutes, or until the soufflés have risen and have a slight jiggle in the center. The tops should be set and slightly cracked.

8. **Serve Immediately:**
   - Chocolate soufflés should be served immediately after baking while they are still puffed and warm. Dust with powdered sugar if desired, and serve with a dollop of whipped cream or a scoop of vanilla ice cream.

Tips:

- **Preparation:** Make sure your mixing bowls and utensils are completely clean and free of grease when beating the egg whites, as any fat can prevent them from whipping up properly.
- **Timing:** Soufflés should be served immediately after baking as they will begin to deflate after a few minutes.
- **Chocolate:** Use high-quality chocolate for the best flavor. You can also experiment with different types of chocolate, such as dark, milk, or a mix.

This chocolate soufflé recipe will give you a light, airy dessert with a rich chocolate flavor that is sure to impress. Enjoy!

Cream Puffs

Ingredients:

For the Choux Pastry:

- 1 cup water
- ½ cup unsalted butter
- 1 cup all-purpose flour
- ¼ teaspoon salt
- 4 large eggs

For the Filling:

- 1 cup heavy cream
- 2 tablespoons granulated sugar
- 1 teaspoon vanilla extract

For the Chocolate Sauce (optional):

- 4 oz semisweet or bittersweet chocolate, chopped
- ¼ cup heavy cream
- 1 tablespoon light corn syrup (optional, for shine)

Instructions:

1. **Prepare the Choux Pastry:**
   - Preheat your oven to 425°F (220°C). Line a baking sheet with parchment paper.
   - In a medium saucepan, bring the water and butter to a boil over medium heat, stirring occasionally.
   - Once boiling, remove from heat and quickly stir in the flour and salt. Mix until the dough pulls away from the sides of the pan and forms a ball.
   - Let the dough cool for about 5 minutes. Then, beat in the eggs one at a time, making sure each egg is fully incorporated before adding the next. The dough should be smooth and glossy.
   - Transfer the dough to a piping bag fitted with a large round or star tip. Pipe 1 to 1.5-inch rounds onto the prepared baking sheet, spacing them about 2 inches apart.
   - Bake for 10 minutes at 425°F (220°C), then reduce the temperature to 350°F (175°C) and bake for an additional 15-20 minutes, or until the puffs are golden brown and crisp. Do not open the oven door during baking.
   - Let the puffs cool completely on a wire rack.
2. **Prepare the Filling:**
   - In a medium bowl, whip the heavy cream, granulated sugar, and vanilla extract until stiff peaks form. You can use an electric mixer for this.
   - Transfer the whipped cream to a piping bag fitted with a small round tip.

3. **Fill the Cream Puffs:**
   - Once the puffs are completely cooled, use a small knife to cut a small slit in the side of each puff.
   - Pipe the whipped cream into each puff until it is filled.
4. **Prepare the Chocolate Sauce (optional):**
   - In a small saucepan, heat the cream over medium heat until it begins to simmer.
   - Pour the hot cream over the chopped chocolate in a heatproof bowl. Let it sit for 1-2 minutes, then stir until smooth. Stir in the corn syrup if using.
   - Let the chocolate sauce cool slightly before drizzling over the filled cream puffs.
5. **Serve:**
   - Arrange the filled cream puffs on a serving platter.
   - Drizzle with chocolate sauce or dust with powdered sugar if desired.

Tips:

- **Choux Pastry:** Ensure that the dough is fully mixed before adding the eggs. The dough should be thick but pipeable.
- **Filling Variations:** You can also fill cream puffs with pastry cream, custard, or ice cream if you prefer.
- **Storage:** Cream puffs are best enjoyed the same day they are filled. If storing, keep them in an airtight container in the refrigerator.

Cream puffs are versatile and can be made with various fillings and toppings to suit your taste. Enjoy your delicious homemade cream puffs!

Gingerbread Cookies

Ingredients:

For the Cookies:

- 3 ¼ cups all-purpose flour
- 1 teaspoon baking soda
- 1 tablespoon ground ginger
- 1 tablespoon ground cinnamon
- ½ teaspoon ground cloves
- ¼ teaspoon salt
- ¾ cup unsalted butter, softened
- ½ cup granulated sugar
- ½ cup packed brown sugar
- 1 large egg
- ¾ cup molasses

For the Royal Icing (optional, for decorating):

- 2 large egg whites
- 4 cups powdered sugar
- 1 teaspoon lemon juice or white vinegar

Instructions:

1. **Prepare the Dough:**
   - In a medium bowl, whisk together the flour, baking soda, ginger, cinnamon, cloves, and salt.
   - In a large bowl, cream together the softened butter, granulated sugar, and brown sugar until light and fluffy.
   - Beat in the egg and molasses until well combined.
   - Gradually add the dry ingredients to the butter mixture, mixing until just combined. The dough will be thick.
2. **Chill the Dough:**
   - Divide the dough into two equal parts, flatten into disks, and wrap in plastic wrap. Refrigerate for at least 1 hour, or overnight. Chilling helps the dough firm up and makes it easier to roll out.
3. **Roll and Cut the Cookies:**
   - Preheat your oven to 350°F (175°C). Line baking sheets with parchment paper.
   - On a lightly floured surface, roll out one disk of dough to about ¼-inch thickness. Use cookie cutters to cut out shapes and transfer them to the prepared baking sheets.
   - Gather scraps, re-roll, and cut out additional shapes.
4. **Bake the Cookies:**

- Bake in the preheated oven for 8-10 minutes, or until the edges are firm but the centers are still soft. The cookies will firm up as they cool.
- Allow the cookies to cool on the baking sheets for a few minutes before transferring to a wire rack to cool completely.

5. **Decorate (Optional):**
    - To make royal icing, beat the egg whites until frothy, then gradually add powdered sugar and lemon juice or vinegar, beating until stiff peaks form.
    - Transfer the icing to piping bags or squeeze bottles and decorate the cooled cookies as desired. Allow the icing to dry completely before storing.

Tips:

- **Spices:** Adjust the spice levels to your taste. For a spicier cookie, add a little more ginger or cloves.
- **Rolling Out Dough:** If the dough is too sticky, chill it a bit longer or lightly flour your rolling surface and rolling pin.
- **Cutouts:** If you're using intricate cookie cutters, lightly flour them to help prevent sticking.

These gingerbread cookies are perfect for holiday gatherings, cookie exchanges, or just enjoying with a cup of tea or milk. Enjoy baking and decorating!

Custard

Ingredients:

- 2 cups whole milk
- ½ cup granulated sugar
- 4 large egg yolks
- 1 teaspoon vanilla extract
- A pinch of salt

Instructions:

1. **Heat the Milk:**
   - In a medium saucepan, heat the milk over medium heat until it begins to steam but does not boil. You should see small bubbles around the edges. Remove from heat.
2. **Prepare the Egg Mixture:**
   - In a medium bowl, whisk the egg yolks with the granulated sugar and a pinch of salt until the mixture is pale and slightly thickened.
3. **Temper the Eggs:**
   - Gradually pour a small amount of the hot milk into the egg yolk mixture while whisking constantly. This process, called tempering, helps to gently raise the temperature of the eggs without scrambling them.
   - Slowly add the remaining hot milk to the egg mixture, whisking constantly.
4. **Cook the Custard:**
   - Return the combined mixture to the saucepan. Cook over medium-low heat, stirring constantly with a wooden spoon or heat-resistant spatula, until the custard thickens enough to coat the back of the spoon. This should take about 5-8 minutes. Do not allow the mixture to boil, as this can cause curdling.
5. **Strain and Flavor:**
   - Once thickened, remove the custard from heat and strain it through a fine-mesh sieve into a clean bowl to remove any curdled bits or impurities.
   - Stir in the vanilla extract.
6. **Cool and Serve:**
   - Allow the custard to cool slightly before transferring it to serving dishes. If you're serving it chilled, cover the surface of the custard with plastic wrap to prevent a skin from forming.
   - Chill in the refrigerator for at least 2 hours before serving.

Tips:

- **Consistency:** If you accidentally overcook the custard and it curdles, you can try blending it with an immersion blender to smooth it out, though it's best to avoid this if possible.

- **Flavor Variations:** You can infuse the milk with different flavors by heating it with ingredients like cinnamon sticks, vanilla beans, or citrus zest, and then straining before adding to the egg mixture.
- **Using Custard:** This basic vanilla custard can be used in a variety of desserts, including custard tarts, as a filling for pastries, or as a topping for fruit.

Custard is a versatile and classic dessert that's both comforting and elegant. Enjoy your homemade custard!